Papa's Legacy
The Growing of
GRANDchildren

Live with joy!

Jan Fleming

PAPA'S LEGACY
THE GROWING *of*
GRANDCHILDREN

Joan
Fleming

Beaver's Pond Press, Inc.

Edina, Minnesota

Editor: Barbara J. Winter
Production Supervisor: Milton Adams
Design & Format: Jaana Bykonich, Mori Studio

ISBN 1-890676-65-9

Library of Congress Catalog Number: 00-105735

First Printing: July 2000
Printed in the United States of America

03 02 01 00 5 4 3 2 1

*For My Family Circle and
the Generations That Will Follow*

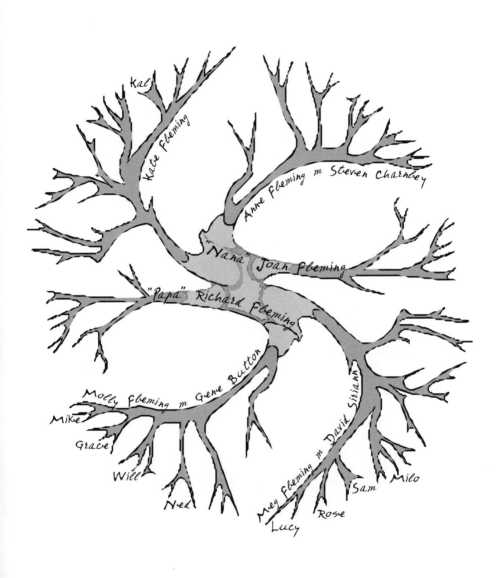

TABLE OF CONTENTS

INTRODUCTION
....xi

CHAPTER ONE
  THE FLAMBEAU STORIES 1

CHAPTER TWO
  PAPA AND HIS DAUGHTERS...13
    The Family Trivia Game 14
    The Family Letter 17
    The Christmas Letter...21
    A Grain of Salt 23
    Papa's Recipes 24

CHAPTER THREE
  PAPA AND HIS GRANDCHILDREN...27
    Papa's Bootcamp 28
    Letters 35
    Goalsetting with Grandchildren 40
    The Fleming Family Theater Troupe 42
    The Script for the Thanksgiving Play..............................46
    Kenny at the River with Mike and Papa Dick...................48
    The Treasure Hunt...50
    Kal's Report on the Treasure Hunt 53
    Tarps and Bungi Cords 54
    An Outhouse to the Rescue 55
    Miniature Log House 56
    Papa Dick and Nana's Audiotapes 56
    A Fleming Fourth of July 59

CHAPTER FOUR

GRANDMOTHER'S ZESTS 63
    My Eclectic Eccentric Dollhouse 64
    The Loon on a Lake Table 65
    Paper Dolls with Pizazz 66
    The Steamer Trunk 66
    Pillowcases and Placemats 68
    Photo Albums Every Christmas 69
    Yearly Photo Day 69
    Imagination Boxes 70

CHAPTER FIVE

PASSING THE TORCH 73
    At Granny's Side 74
    Garden Soup 75
    The Artists of Everyday Life 79
    Kal's Treasure Hunt 81

AFTERWORD

....85

WITH APPRECIATION

....87

ABOUT THE AUTHOR

....89

I'D LOVE TO HEAR FROM YOU

....91

Introduction

Family stories are the heart of *Papa's Legacy*. Every family worldwide has stories to cherish, but, as often happens, their memorable value remains contained within the family. The telling of *Papa's Legacy* is meant to inspire and fortify a collective voice of experience. It is a book about the purposeful sharing of one generation's wisdom and love with another generation through the experiences of Papa Dick and his eight (soon to be nine) grandchildren. Out of this storytelling emerges many of the enduring qualities of life: sense of tradition, belonging, values, confidence and fun. It is in the spirit of fun and joy that I offer these stories.

As of this writing, I have been married to Papa Dick for forty-six years. We have four daughters: Anne, Kate, Meg and Molly. Our sons-in-law are Steven (Anne), David (Meg), and Gene (Molly). When we became grandparents (beginning in 1988, with steady contributions through 1994), we were inspired to revisit childhood through the eyes of our grandchildren. Being removed one generation from the responsibilities of parenthood we discovered what fun these young people can be.

We knew, as well, that there are lasting effects on a child's self-confidence that finds its origin in loving elders. When children know that they are loved unconditionally by their parents and extended family, and that in their grandparents' eyes they are perfect just as they are, they have a powerful resource that helps them move with enthusiasm toward their dreams. Equally important, they become men and women who can express and accept love.

In the workshops I conduct, I talk about living with a sense of purpose–something of your own choosing that gives your life greater meaning and pleasure. I find as I talk with others that a sense of purpose almost always means making a difference in the lives of others. However, living "on purpose" doesn't just happen. Finding those things that greatly increase quality of life is a challenging process of reflecting about what is important now, listening to our inner voices with self-confidence, and living the values that we say are meaningful to us. I also believe that it means being aware of the ways our lives influence the lives of others–both positively and negatively. If we can sense and respond to the needs others have, we can live with abundance.

When I'm doing a *Seven Habits of Highly Effective People* workshop, I talk at the close about Dr. Stephen Covey's *Seven Sources of Personal Strength*. I spend an increasing amount of time with the value placed on extended family. The people in my workshops talk with great enthusiasm about childhood memories and the people who were most influential in their early lives. We talk about what we would like to experience in our families now. Many times people begin to design zestful plans for their children and grandchildren. Those who seldom experienced joyful times because of painful childhoods know that they can create for their own families — now — the fun they missed as children. The choices that these people are making fulfill my sense of purpose dramatically.

Papa's Legacy exists to help you add to the legacy of fun and discovery in your own extended family. Use and adapt the ideas freely–and add your own personal touches. After all, what greater gift do we have to share with each other than the wisdom gained through years of life experience?

Chapter One
The Flambeau Stories

It's the English who think time is a straight line which can be divided up and parceled out in an orderly fashion, but time isn't like that. Time is a circle, time goes round and round like a wheel and that's why one hears echoes from the past continually...it's because the past is present: you don't have to look back down the straight line, you just look across the circle and there are echoes of the past and the vision of the future. And they're all present, all now...all forever.

from The Wheel of Fortune
by Susan Howatch

Do you have a "sense of place"? A place where you became more comfortable with yourself because of the love you experienced and the encouragement you received when you were there? A place of belonging?

Some people feel that way about the home they grew up in; for others, it was a place away from home. Either way, it's a place where, many years later, you can still travel to in your mind. It's a place you'd like to tell those you love about so that they might come to know you better.

Papa Dick has such a place. You could find it on a map of Wisconsin. It's located near the Flambeau River in the northern part of the state. More specifically, it's at a bend in the river called the Oxbo because of its shape. There was a cabin there sitting in a clearing so the river was visible. If you looked down towards the river on the left you would see a gigantic white pine tree that's still standing there. The cabin, however, was torn down some years ago so all that remains is a meadow. When Papa Dick walked in the meadow he said he heard echoes from the past.

Papa Dick

Papa Dick spent the summers of his youth in this magical place surrounded by three exceptional adults: his great-grand-mother Ida, Ida's sister Kate and Ida's son Uncle Ferd. Perhaps without even realizing it, these people laid the foundation for the man Papa Dick would become and taught him the values he holds dear today.

Our daughter Kate, who teaches creative writing classes, is convinced that "memory writing" is the most valuable and necessary writing we all can do. Obviously, her father agrees. In 1989, Papa Dick wrote a collection of recollections about his days on the Flambeau River to give as a Christmas gift to his daughters and their children (and, hopefully, their future children). Frequently, during family gatherings, they are asked for and told again. Everyone understands the meaning of a Flambeau.

I hope as you read these pages, you'll recall with tenderness the people from your childhood who nourished you. Here are some excerpts from those Flambeau Stories which illustrate why those experiences made such an impression on Papa Dick as a young boy.

This is a daunting project. I am setting out to tell many stories of long ago. I do have my memories, but they are massaged and eroded by time and, for sure, affected by the love I still feel for Uncle Ferd, his mother Ida, and her sister Kate. I intend to pay little regard to the truth or more accurately said, the facts, for I don't want to become bogged down when the real message of these recollections has to do with bonds, the surges of childhood, the events which are today blurred, but still come back simply as smells, tingles, sounds, human touch and, always, anticipation. You will see, I think, why it was an exciting place for a six-year-old!

We have a deep and treasured resource in this family. It is our closeness, our interest and caring in what each other is doing- thinking-enduring-enjoying. I think this is mostly due to Joan's valuing such ties, but more than that, taking action both by her example and by steering and causing togetherness to happen. As in most worthwhile events, somebody has to do something, and she has. Fortunately, the rest of us fall into line, for we discover that we thrive when together. Yep, I do, too, even though my tolerance level for chaos seems to be narrowing.

Part of the reason we fall in line is that we act according to our values and those values were built early on. In my case, a good dose of that took place via my Flambeau associations. Ferd, Ida, and Kate all loved me dearly. I knew it then and I know it now and that single knowledge colors and enriches the daily events of the past and, most certainly, of the present.

So these Flambeau Stories are a means of passing the torch-perhaps of delving mysteriously into who and what we are and, just possibly, where we are going. I hope so. I would like that.

Ferdinand Julius Derge, brother of my grandfather Herman, was the Lord of Dergehaven Lodge. I use the term loosely as Great-grandmother Ida, along with her sister Kate, were the power and balance of the place.

When I was six years old, Ferd was about fifty. For some reason, I never thought of Ferd as being any certain age, unlike all other grownups who seemed ancient to me. Ferd was my companion. We were into things together and we consulted freely back and forth with mutual respect. It doesn't matter to me now (and certainly not then) that Ferd was emotionally disturbed. He had a series of nervous breakdowns over a number of years. I am told that he was a manic-depressive, which in today's jargon is bi-polar something or other.

Ferd had a fine education and was both an electrical and mechanical engineer. He invented some things (I don't know what really), but he was a creative, ingenious person. Then his mental problems began, resulting in his early retirement. All of that laid the groundwork for his fleeing to the north woods of Wisconsin where he lived with his mother for the rest of his life. Thus began Dergehaven Lodge. The cabin was located about a half mile from the Oxbo Resort on the Flambeau River.

Then there was my great-grandmother Ida, or Ade as Kate most often addressed her. She is my notion of whatever the best things are that a grandma could be. She was tiny, even to me as a child, and in spite of that was a powerful force-a force for good. Everyday she wore a small flower print dress covered by an apron made out of a Robin Hood flour sack. Her one bit of jewelry was a cameo brooch. She progressed with a forward lean and a bit of a sag and, I would have to say, shuffled more than walked. Her slippers made a *swoosh, swoosh ,swoosh* on the linoleum floor of the kitchen and this was overlaid by a thoughtful semi-whistle that fell just short of a real whistle. (To get a better idea of this, purse your lips fairly tightly, think of a tune like *Merrily We Roll Along* and "blow it" across your lips so that only you can sense the tune. If you do this, someone close to you will also hear it and then you'll know what I'm trying to say about Ida). She did this a lot and it was cheerful and comforting.

Ida's main beat was the kitchen where she presided as boss. She had a wood stove and later, next to it, an electric stove. She would not part with her wood stove! The electric stove was the newest thing and she always remarked how nice it was to have it, although as far as I could tell, it was only used to keep things warm that had been properly prepared on "old faithful".

Ferd used to tease her by pulling woodticks off his dog, Duke, and throwing them on the hot surface of the wood stove. They would swell up nicely like an expanding grape and sometimes pop or hiss. I used to throw ticks on the stove, too, but tried to only do so when she was not watching. It just wasn't fair or fun to tease her. I would never knowingly tease or in any way purposely hurt Grandma. She was my refuge, my warm place, my absolutely predictable champion and she would tickle my back endlessly.

In the evenings, after supper and before dark, we often went to the porch and experienced quiet time. Ferd would play some musical selections on his Zenith radio, re-study the day's mail, or read his papers. Grandma had her own rocking chair and she'd call me over to snuggle in her lap, cover me with a shawl and tickle my back. The fading sun hit on the far bank of the river across from us and frequently a deer or several deer would come to the river to drink. It was lazy and peaceful and then she would tell me stories. I can't remember a single story now. They were all made up on the spot and whatever they meant, the story itself was not so important. It was more a matter of being together there–of being safe and warm and content.

5

There were two sights upriver that were constant, that were friends, and that always made me feel whole. One was a large rock that stuck out of the water in the middle of the river and past the rock on Ferd's property was a white pine tree on the water's edge. You might think it odd that a tree would be so strong in memory, but not if you saw this tree. And you can! On July 3, 1989 Joan and I drove from our cottage to the Flambeau. I followed the old road which is not now in use for there is a new bridge down the stream from the old. We parked just short of the old bridge–still there but grown smaller–and walked to the middle of that bridge. I saw the rock, *my rock*, and—Oh my God!—the white pine standing over all! I hear that "nothing is forever", but that is enough for me. Fifty years have passed and my friends are still there.

My education at the Flambeau took many forms. Some forces entirely out of my control (you may be assured of that) determined that I would listen to music, sit in conversations about music, carry doughnuts and coffee to folks gathered to hear music, and sort of generally admit music actively into my life. Abe Ruvinsky, concert violinist, was almost a summer resident. Abe took a shine to me. He called me Bubbie which was, I think, a Russian term of endearment. It just kind of grew that I was going to be a violinist, and that goal was launched very vigorously with two lessons a day.

After a time, Ferd hatched a brilliant idea. "Let's build a conservatory. A place that's dedicated to music!" So we did. It was a log building situated on the far corner of the property in a grove of white pine trees. Ralph Burger, another summer guest, also played the violin. He would sit in on my lessons at least once a day. Then he had an idea. "LET'S HAVE A RECITAL!" I put capitals on those words because, let me tell you, when the full meaning of what this was all about came to my mind it really got my attention! This darned thing just went beyond all reason and before long we had made some very large size arrangements.

Down at the main road, below the mailbox and between it and the bridge at the river, on the opposite side of the road, was a large log building with a gas pump in front. It had a big white crown on the top of it. In the back of this building was a large rectangular room, almost like my first grade school room. It may once have been a school. That was the site of the recital.

Invitations were hand lettered and sent to everyone far and wide. I mean dozens of people: the Behrendt's, the Feleen's, the Johnsons, Pete Saber, Oscar Rude, Loretta and Marie, Joe and Faye Bower, my buddies Ahkey and Elmer, Verna Neubauer and her mother, Jenny, Moses, Boyd from Mason Lake and his crew, and those are just the ones I knew from our usual rounds. There were people I never even saw before!

The performers were listed: I was Master Richard Fleming, Student, and the others were Abe and Burger. The selections were indicated along with who was to play, and the composer. They were folded and had a ribbon inside. They were elegant.

Ida and Kate were in charge of the lunch. A large number of folding chairs came from the town hall in Draper and the stage was set. This was absolutely my first step on the public stage and for days before and right up to the last minute of the appointed day with its first uncertain note, life was excruciating. In the days prior to the big day, nothing else was in my mind except the imminent disaster and my suffocating death before all those people.

Finally, the big day arrived. The guests were all in their finest garb and suitably respectful of the great symphony artist and conductor. Ferd was the introducer and on his best behavior. He wore a vest with a gold chain and from the chain his keys of professional distinction and his pocket watch.

I wasn't first, but pretty early in the show. I played *Minuet in G* all by myself and Burger and I played something called *Cielito Lindo* and that was a duet. Come to think of it, I think I did *The Merry Widow Waltz* as well. When I finished there was thunderous applause and I returned to my seat in relief. Burger put his arm around me and gave me a squeeze. He smiled at me. A smile from Burger was a message from his soul. I have to say it was a glorious recital and I'm glad we only did it one time.

It would be hard for any other person to know Ferd as I knew him. Perhaps we all have a personal and private "knowing" as to what another looks like, acts like, is. The visible signs and actions are there for all to behold but filtered through our own reality. My description of Ferd is sharply colored by my understanding that he loved me, that he considered my point of view, that we approached daily assignments as a team.

His facade offered some valuable clues to his inner self. Most often he wore a canvas cap with a plastic visor set square on his head and he looked determined. His face was full and kind and set off by wire-rimmed glasses and a faint stubble of beard. He wore woolen knickers with suspenders over a checked flannel shirt and carried several pens in the pocket along with his Marvel cigarettes. The cigarettes were burned in a black cigarette holder with a silver band around the end. It often served as a tool in driving home his views. The knickers were tucked into leather knee boots. When conditions required, he knotted two corners of a large bandanna and placed it over his head, under his cap so it flowed over his neck and unto his back. This was mostly for mosquito protection, but I suspect it also was used to complete his public appearance.

When not agitated, his eyes revealed interest and this was affirmed by a frequent smile that said, "It's OK." When agitated, however, there was no doubt; his eyes would flash and dart and, at the worst, would roll up in his head and his voice and behavior was just short of a tantrum.This was accompanied by redness and flying spit. This happened most often when discussing politics.

Ferd had a black Chrysler coupe. It was a two-door model and I don't think there was a back seat. If there was, it had been removed and so had the back wall of the interior so that it was all open space from the front seat to the very back of the trunk. He had placed an old mattress in that rear space and that's where I would frequently ride along with his springer spaniel and constant companion Duke.

Amidst occasional quiet spells, we visited about a wide variety of subjects. Some of these discussions had form and sense, but many were flights of fancy. Occasionally, our substance would really deteriorate to the point of wild laughter and/or giggling, followed by moments of pulling together, then a repeat of the key word, and again, shrieks and shakes. When the notion took him, he would say, "Isn't that the beat of it!" This wasn't really a question and did not require an answer; it was a sort of rhetorical wonderment, though there were variations, always said with a certain tone and inflection. "Isn't that the beat of it!" This phrase was not part of normal conversation and seemed to be a sort of bandage or medication after things had gotten seriously out of control. To me, it advised that we were about to go on to other things.

Sometimes on the way to Fifield, never on any basis I could predict, Ferd would detour off the blacktop and down a long, narrow dirt road and I'd know we were heading for Zirngable's place.

Zirngable was also known as Moses and thus he appeared. He was kind of a cross between your view of Moses and Ben Gunn from *Treasure Island*. He lived alone without human companionship, but had a stable of various beasts–some penned and some in the wild. His home was a hovel, a tarpaper shack with appendages constructed from scraps and oddments which he transported in the bed of his sick truck. Chickens ran every which way. As near as I can tell, Ferd went there to hone his political views and to practice his worst, most maniacal behavior. Most often the discussion erupted in violence and one or the other would beat on the hood of the car. We never went inside his place. This was, I think, for the best. I really did worry because Ferd would get in such a state of frenzy that our trip back to the road was often abrupt and dangerously reckless. All the way he repeated the sense of his case and pleaded for my endorsement. I was only too glad to please and usually by the time we got back to the blacktop his neck was again flesh color and he would say, "Isn't that the beat of it!" And everything would be OK.

Did you ever hear of a shivaree? A shivaree is something that all the friends and acquaintances do to get a new marriage started right. The dictionary calls it "a serenade for newlyweds." Secrecy and surprise are major elements; darkness is advised; and you must know the sleeping location of the newlyweds. Then you need some other props as well: noisemakers, firecrackers, roman candles — anything that will make a wild and raucous clamor, including banshee screams and beating on kitchen pans with wooden spoons. This thing proceeds in phases, with the final phase being the snatching of the love pair from their nest and engaging in a no-holds-barred feast.

A young couple over at the Hanson's place had gotten married. The Hansons were one of the oldest settlers in the area. They had come as homesteaders and their first living quarters consisted of a dugout burrowed into the ground and lined with fresh cut timbers. It was completely earth covered except for the south facing entrance toward the Flambeau River. It had a hole in the middle and a chimney, of sorts, fired by a small barrel stove. There were no windows. The first Hansons lived–endured–there and their clan grew from that beginning.

Anyway, the word went out that the shivaree was set
for Tuesday night and a rallying point was set up. All
were to gather there, then, in most careful silence, pro-
ceed to surround the corner bedroom of their small cabin
where the innocent couple had already retired. It was a
potluck affair. I don't remember what we took, but I do
know that I was to take a copper washtub and fill it with
soda and to ice down our limited supply. So we gathered
with great, good cheer. After lots of plotting we departed
furtively in a string of various darkened vehicles with
each one having their assignment. I understood that I
was to join the crowd, to take my dishpan and then,
when the signal was given, to pound furiously, making
as much noise as possible while at the same time scream-
ing, barking, howling at my most creative peak! That's
all I knew; it wasn't clear why we were doing this, but it
didn't matter. I was willing.

Our leader waved us to a halt followed by gesturing
and gesticulating overlaid by hoarse whispers and muf-
fled laughter and, here and there, muted flashlights. I
suppose there were forty people or so, folks of all ages
including some babes in arms and our team–Ferd, Ida,
Kate and me–right in the middle.

Then there was a thunderous explosion. It could have
been dynamite–and probably was–and all hell broke
loose! Fireworks whistling, pots banging, a din of
pounding and scraping metals, hollers and hoots, and
just generally an earthshaking wave that went on for
many minutes, then ebbed, then caught fire once more
and then a multitude of cheers, applause and high-spirited
good cries hard to decipher, but clear in meaning: the
bride and groom had joined us.

Soon thereafter, the fixens were spread, all outside on
and surrounding the porch. Lanterns were produced and
a feast ensued. There was good cheer wherever you
turned — that is my clearest memory. Here and there,
youngsters formerly unknown to each other would
break new ground, become friends, then pick up their

noise tools and set off another mini-display. All this was encouraged or, at the very least, not curtailed.

Do you know what a flambeau is? It is a flaming torch. Just below the double trunk, and now fifteen feet or so from the ground, you can still see scars in the trunk of the pine tree I love. Scars where, long before Ferd's time, flaming torches were lit and placed, stuck in the tree to guide the night passage of those on the river. That haunts me. This tree was mine in my place of guidance and it is still there now, fifty years later. And so am I. I hope these Flambeau stories will light your passage, and yours, after you pass along.

CHAPTER *Two*
PAPA AND HIS DAUGHTERS

*You define your identity by having it reflected
back by someone who shares your memories.*

— UNKNOWN

Papa Dick's Flambeau Stories fell on fertile soil with our
daughters. The stories gave them more insight into the man
their father is. If today they see him as fearless, they now know
that he felt performance anxiety as a young boy giving a violin
recital, not unlike some of their own experiences. His grandson
Sam anxiously practiced and awaited the day of his own piano
recital only to feel, as the day grew near, that it was something he
would rather not do. It was Sam's responsibility to call his piano
teacher. He made three phone calls: the first two to give his
excuses as to why he'd be absent and the last one to say he
would honor his responsibility. Later, Papa Dick read again to
Sam about his own feelings concerning the violin recital so many
years before and Sam realized his experience was much like that
of his grandfather. Furthermore, they both triumphed.

Like all parents raising families, we experienced the ups and
downs, highs and lows. We had ordinary days that now flow
together in our minds leaving few conscious memories. There are
also the joys we don't ever want to forget. There's the sense that
life will always be the way it is today and then the crashing real-
ization of how fast the days become years. Then there are the fric-
tions between budding and entrenched egos and the tensions that
replace the longed for harmony.

I cannot say it better than our daughter Kate did in a birthday poem she wrote to Dick during her high school years.

Though it may not always be clear
The things that are most
Important in life
I've learned from you.
And sometimes the presence of fear-
Your reaction to the things that I do
A crunch of a pickle
An overspent nickel
A stolen condiment
An unspoken sentiment
Makes it hard to communicate
On a level that's true.

So when I say it's black
And you say it's blue
While I'm finding my way
Sometimes I forget... you are, too.

I think sometimes about what holds a family together and it seems to me that a family and a home have much in common. If the bricks of a family are common values and the mortar is a collection of family events that brings smiles and fond memories, the storms caused by our human weaknesses don't stand much of a chance.

In our family we invented a number of shared activities that tapped into old memories and created new ones. There were four experiences, in particular, that gave our family a stronger sense of belonging, of being a family.

Family Trivia Game

Here's a family game that you can use in your own family to recall moments that have meaning to you. Sometime in the autumn about eight years ago, Dick asked our daughters and sons-in-law to get some 3 X 5 cards and then on each one write a question that had to do with their family memories. Dick and I would do the same and Dick would talk to his mother and encourage her stories. If the person knew the answer they were to write it on the back of the card, but if they didn't, that was fine, too. Someone else in the family would know the answer. If everyone in the family writes about ten questions you have the makings of a good game.

We played Family Trivia one evening during our Christmas time together. I read the cards and each person took turns giving their response. The answer wasn't nearly as important as the conversation that flowed. "Tell us more!" was a frequent response.

This game can become increasingly exciting when older family members ask questions and tell stories that the younger generation haven't heard.

To give you some ideas, I'll share three of our family stories about our ancestors.

QUESTION: What were the circumstances under which Lizette Sunderman came to the United States from Germany?

ANSWER: Lizette was my father's mother and my grandfather literally kidnapped her just before he was to board a ship to this country. She was promised to his younger brother, but my grandfather had other plans! Did my grandmother agree to the kidnapping? Did the brothers ever speak again? These intriguing questions remain unanswered.

QUESTION: What happened to Great, Great Aunt Rose?

ANSWER: Papa Dick's Great, Great Aunt lived in Boston and was born into a very proper family. Rose fell in love with a traveling salesman who was known as a smooth talker. She followed the man out West where, to her horror, she found he was already a bigamist. Her despair led her to throw herself down a well where she died. Apparently, it was the lesser of two evils–the other being telling her parents. Not a very uplifting story, but it is part of our history.

QUESTION: On what island was Joan's grandmother Natalie born and raised?

ANSWER: The Isle of Sylt, off the coast of Germany. There was no one living in my mother's family that could tell me about the hotel my grandparents had on Sylt. On impulse, I wrote to the Burgermeister on the island to ask for any information available on my family. I didn't really expect a reply. A few months later a thick envelope arrived containing my grandmother's birth certificate, a large brochure about the Isle of Sylt, and an old photo of their hotel. What made me a further believer in genetics was that in the photo and next to their hotel was a gazebo. I have loved gazebos for as long as I can remember and the year before one was built next to our home.

Questions don't need to have a story connected to them. Sometimes a simple question about a memory ignites a round of laughter. One such favorite is this: "What did Kate say when she was three years old and found a dirty piece of candy lying in the grass?" I was hanging up laundry when she came running to me and said, "Look what Jesus threw down for me!"

Another is "What was the meaning of 'ga-ga', 'goo-goo', according to two-year-old Lucy?" When I was playing with a small set of animals with Lucy, she would pick one up and tell me by feeling it what it was. "Nana, this is bear." "Nana, this is monkey." "Nana, this is duck." I told her that the first word I ever said was duck, and I asked her what the first word she ever said was. She answered "Ga-ga, goo-goo." I leaned closer and asked, "What does ga-ga, goo- goo mean?" In a flicker of an eyelash she said, "It means hello…in Spanish!"

Lucy's father David thinks it would be a grand idea to have a kid's trivia game during the coming year. The children would ask the questions and the adults would attempt answers. Knowing the sometimes devious and ingenious turns their fruitful minds can take, I think we're headed for another memorable event.

However you adapt this game, it always opens the door to conversation that includes all members of the family.

The Family Letter

Many of you have letters in your possession that mean as much to you as favorite family photographs, letters that reveal the nature of people and relationships, letters that bring back a flood of memories. We have such a letter that is cherished.

Early in their marriage, my father used to leave little notes for my mother in the mailbox. Since they were rarely parted, it seemed there was never a good time for my mother to respond, although she always said she would — someday. As destiny would have it, she was inspired to write about a year before her unexpected death. I was aware of the letter, as were my sister and brother, but we were never given the letter to read. Our father died a year after my mother and in the weeks that followed, we had the heart-rending task of cleaning out our family home and either distributing or disposing of its contents. Anyone who has had this experience will understand the avalanche of feelings and sadness that overwhelms you. Then we remembered the letter. Suddenly there was a focus and a search. Nothing seemed more important — no object, thing or photo — than finding that letter! It is in my care now and it will live as a reminder of their devotion and love for each other and their children.

Many years later, when three of our four daughters were attending colleges, the idea of a family letter came to my mind. I discussed this with Papa Dick. Since my own record of letter writing was pathetic, the idea of a family letter probably came through layers of guilt and devotion to the telephone. The purpose of our family letter in the beginning was to cut down on the phone bills, which insured Papa Dick's enthusiastic cooperation.

We'd heard of "round robin" letters but rejected that idea because of too much stale news by the time it made its rounds. I sat at a typewriter and together we produced the format:

Fleming Family Support Group and Weekly Update
What were this week's highlights?
What was one thing you learned?
Did you help make someone else's life a little better?

Did you experience any "downer" you'd like to get off your chest?
Anything by way of exercise or physical activity?
When were you most pleased with yourself?
Any new goals? Want any help with following through?

We talked with our daughters about giving this idea a try and asked that they write their responses to any questions that fit, ignoring those that didn't apply on any certain week. If they had more to write, they could turn the form letter over. In an effort to have a successful start, I gave them several copies of the form along with stamped envelopes. We told them that we would answer the same questions and when their letters arrived, I'd make duplicates and send each of their three sisters copies along with Dick's and my letters. We would keep all of the originals, including our own. Although we weren't aware of this when we started it soon became apparent that we were writing a family journal.

Don't think of our family letter as a "Walton family experience" without the fits and starts of a fairly normal group of people who live in the real world. We found that it was easier to write when life was going smoothly and difficult if we were going through a painful period or simply feeling lethargic. Seeking each other's approval was, I believe, an issue as important to Papa Dick and me as it was for the four girls. Yet when either Papa Dick or I wrote about a "downer", our daughters came to know us better.

We also learned that writing the letters once a week became a real drag, especially for the person standing over the copy machine. We tried every two weeks and then, better yet, we simply put a due date on our letters. We neglected to write when we were spending time together or over the holidays. Looking back, I miss not having a written record of these important times.

I sometimes think of these letters as forming a crazy quilt–a crazy family quilt made up of the little adventures, the ups and downs, of daily life and the relationships that these letters strengthened.

A few years ago we shortened the letter. It now includes:

Highlights of the last few weeks.
Information to pass around: book recommendations,
exciting new recipes, anything of interest.
News of the grandchildren or messages for them.

One of Papa Dick's ideas was to include a space for the grand-children to write a note or draw a picture. We also found some great suggestions from other family letters.

It's hard to be humble... tell us of some of your recent
accomplishments.
Current events. Current laments.
For the benefit of a new spouse, tell something you
remember from their new mate's childhood.
Biggest turn off? Biggest turn on?
What have you done for your mind and what can you
suggest for mine?
What's the latest fad in your area?
Any cultural events you enjoyed?

A further idea is from a family with nine children. The father of these children, all grown and some married, asked them to contribute a paragraph or two that he would then put on his computer. Their input would be part of a newsletter called *Family Chronicle*. Since it is printed once a month, the first page is a calendar with all the birthdays, anniversaries and special events marked. Each person or family has their own logo such as *The Berkley Bunch, Navy Task Force, Paul's Tall Tales* and *The Old Sage*. The Old Sage is the father's ninety-three-year-old mother who tends to recall happenings from her past. In one of their Christmas editions she wrote about her childhood memories of the holiday.

I think sometimes about our grandchildren reading the letters. I visualize an older version of who they are today smiling about their mother's response to a question and then asking them for more detail. I can also picture them shrieking and saying, "Wait till you read this one!" One thing is certain: they will come to know us even better. Just maybe, if they continue to be as close as they are now, one of them will suggest a cousin's letter in the future and keep this lovely tradition going.

A Sampling of Quotes from Our Family Letters

(Helped someone else) *I spent two hours talking to a very depressed friend. Yes, I was in the tub at the time, but she really needed someone to listen.*
— Meg

(Pleased about yourself) *When I didn't fall off my high heels at the dance.*
— Molly

(Goals) *To keep in touch with myself. I see too many people making poor decisions based on the fact that they don't know who they are or what they want.* — Anne

(Goal) *I'm gearing myself up to ask this one guy at school to go out. What can I say? The phrase 'out of the frying pan' comes to mind.* — Meg

(Learned) *I learned that a scholar like Meg has trouble spelling doughnut. Probably less trouble eating them.* — Kate

(Pleased with self) *When I didn't throw up after hearing that Molly is going to model wedding gowns.* — Kate

(Exercise) *I intend to do Jane Fonda exercises — starting tomorrow. I write this with a piece of Canadian bacon caught in my teeth. I'm eating pizza.* —Molly

(Downer) *I was bringing my sheep brain home from school on Friday to study it for the weekend and I left it on the bus.*
— Anne

The Christmas Letter

Searching for the perfect gift for the holidays can bring days of agonizing and second-guessing. One family, tired of the yearly search, came up with a playful solution. The family members pick a name and when they get the name, they also get the person's desired gift — *as initials only*. The challenge then becomes guessing what the initials could possibly represent. *ARC* could mean *A Red Car*. The trick is to get the person, within your budget, a gift using those initials. A woman wrote *TT* on her list. She wanted *Thin Thighs*, but received *Twelve Tennis balls*. Her sister wanted *ABG, A Baby Girl*. She received *A Brown Gerbil*. A brother asked for *ACWTL, A Camera With a Telephoto Lens*. He got *A Cow With a Torn Leg* (stuffed variety). One family member, attempting to be totally different, asked for something with a multitude of initials. He got a can of alphabet soup. If your family is imaginative, this could be a fun way to liven up the annual gift hunt.

Our four daughters had been buying each other gifts for years when Kate suggested — no, *pleaded* — one Christmas that instead of buying a gift that they give each other something that they already had. They were to choose something that they thought would please their sisters with no particular economic value stated. Her idea met with no resistance. When they opened their gifts to each other, I experienced a great lump in my throat for they gave some of their most cherished possessions to one another, making that Christmas especially sentimental.

For years, I was the sole gift purchaser for our daughters, signing the cards, "Love, Mother and Dad." Papa Dick said Christmas shopping didn't fit his role description. Then one year he surprised us all by having fur hats made for us. The hats were made from fur that his friend Kenny had trapped. He didn't realize that all of us were opposed to real fur, but, nonetheless, we truly appreciated his efforts and thoughtfulness. The following year, after the other presents had been opened, he gave each of the girls an envelope. When they opened them, they also discovered a hundred dollar bill, accompanied by this letter:

Dear Anne, Kate, Meg and Molly,

I enjoyed having the fur hats made for you last year and have been thinking of a way I could tickle you again. The $100 is not yours except in the sense of being a trustee. It seems to me that we are all right now on an upper. Things do ebb and flow, but right at this moment we have abundance and strength.

So I ask each of you to use your creative and caring abilities and take the $100 and do for some other person or persons less fortunate. Your choices are limited only by your imagination. After awhile, you may want to discuss what happened with the rest of us, but if you don't feel like that, that's okay, too. The sole stipulation is that you use this money to make another person's existence a little brighter. At first I thought that this was a little crass or intrusive, but the more I thought about it, the more it seemed a good thing to do. And while it's great to have generous thoughts, it is greater to do. So go for it!

The results were as unique as the sisters are. Molly gave her money to a cousin who had been a victim of a house fire, while Kate gave hers to a girl she met on a bus who was in dire need.

Papa Dick has continued his personal gift selection since the year of the hats. Some years he finds treasures in antique stores. He, alone, makes his choices and they are astoundingly good ones. He is always on the lookout for special articles when we enjoy a trip away from home. Another lovely gift he gave to the girls was a framed picture of their four faces which had been painted a few years earlier by an artist. We have the portraits in our home and he had photos taken of them, reduced them in size and framed them in four oval frames within a larger frame, giving each daughter a copy of the pictures.

As they open their gifts from him each year, I am reminded that there is something incredibly special about a father's well-chosen gift to his children that no amount of circling counters in a department store can match.

A Grain of Salt

Papa's Cookbook for His Daughters

The Flambeau Stories were such a hit in our family that Papa Dick was urged to write some more. Since one of his favorite subjects is food and cooking, a cookbook seemed inevitable. Here's how he introduced his cookbook, which he called *A Grain of Salt*.

Whatever I do know about food is rooted in being around a family that was obsessed with food, and hence—from my early days, probably before walking—a major portion of my culturization was exposure to discussions of serious proportions about what to eat, when to eat, where to procure, how to prepare, how to serve, and the nuances and merits surrounding the exquisite detail of each of those issues and very important consequences of all of these matters.

Then I fell in love with Joan and soon was introduced to her tribe where I discovered a constant and pervasive obsession with food. This was evidenced by building travel routes around the location of root beer stands. Evening socializing was tethered to TV trays and frantic raids to the kitchen during commercials. Holidays and family gatherings assembled all at a large dining room table for reception salad, poppy seed cake and home-made pickles.

Guess what I discovered through all of this: I discovered that the whole food drama was a magnet for being close. I liked that and I was drawn to that scene. I see cooking in the global sense as loving and being loved. Thus, when I am officiating, I am, in my way, loving.

Papa's Recipes

Christmas Veggie Marinade

The only thing this has to do with Christmas is that one Christmas we ran short of lettuce but had a collection of other viands. It proved to be a hit, although I must say I wasn't sure where it was going as I put it together. Here's what you do:

Assemble a large can of dark red kidney beans, pitted black olives, green salad olives, lots of fresh or dried basil, thin slices of red onion, crescents of celery, and some hot giardinera mix (use your own judgment here).

Put all this in a stainless steel or glass bowl. Add about one-third cup olive oil to two-thirds cup rice wine vinegar, add salt and ground pepper to taste and a teensy bit of sugar. Mix and refrigerate. If you have some, put in some thin slices of red pepper because it's so pretty.

Pesto

Get a huge bunch of basil from the Farmer's Market. Separate leaves from stems and chop coarsely. Get small containers with tight fitting tops. In a large bowl, place all the chopped basil and add to this finely chopped garlic and lots of it. It's hard to overdo. Pack the basil-garlic mix into your small containers leaving about three-fourth inch head space. Add one-half teaspoon salt per container and fill to cover (you must cover the leaves) with deep flavored olive oil. Poke it with a fork to be sure the oil seeps through the mass, and if necessary, add oil to cover. Put these containers in your freezer. Always have one you are working on in your refrigerator.

This stuff is a tremendous flavor enhancer. For example, make pasta al dente, drain and rinse, put the pasta back in the dried pot, put enough chicken bouillon in the pot so as to wet up the pasta so it won't stick and glop, heat this gently and add a small amount of butter, a chunk of pesto to your taste and, while at a slow heat, spin this up. Now throw in a cup or so of freshly grated parmesan, asiago, gorgonzola or romano cheese and spin once more. EAT! The pesto makes the dish.

You can also make pesto using fresh parsley or cilantro. In the above recipe, once you have the finished masterpiece in your bowl, drizzle some smushed almonds over the top. You get smushed almonds by putting whole almonds in a baggy, laying the baggy on a cutting board and giving it a whack or two with the flat side of your cleaver. You can smush garlic or ginger the same way. I only use a baggy for nuts because they fly too far. As for the odd bits of ginger or garlic fused to the wall, this simply adds character to the kitchen. *Bouquet garni au natural.*

A Weird Way to Cook a Whole Chicken

Get a deep pot and fill it two-thirds with water. In the water put eight or so one-fourth inch discs of fresh ginger, peeled, of course. Add salt. Wash the whole chicken in your sink. Get the water boiling fiercely. Put the chicken in the pot with a fistful of fresh parsley and be sure the chicken is completely immersed. Turn the heat off and tightly cover the pot. Leave the whole works alone and after one hour take the chicken out. You may or may not bone the chicken at this point.

Take a very light olive oil and add to it sesame oil and onion salt. Add, if the spirit takes you, some oregano or maybe a small amount of powered bay leaves. You can see that you can adjust this sauce as you see fit. Eat the chicken lukewarm or cold with a bit of this sauce drizzled over it. You will find that this chicken has a very delicate flavor and texture unlike anything else you could do. It is great on strips of romaine with a bit of fresh parsley over the top and some light mayonnaise sauce with perhaps a touch of curry whipped in on the side. Gosh, I just can't stop here. The permutations are infinite!

Dick's memories of the smells and tastes of food date back to childhood, as they do for all of us. Something he talks about frequently are his Great-grandmother Ida's fry cakes. Filled with homemade plum butter and fried in lard, these fry cakes have the power to transport him back to his Flambeau days.

As a birthday surprise one year, I got the original fry cake recipe from his sister Margaret and she suggested that when I made them, I should dress the way Ida did. With a cotton house dress, slippers that swooshed when I walked and a hair net covering my own hair, I presented my surprise. It was a great success.

Since food plays such an important part in family memories, you might want to make sure that your family favorites are recorded and passed on. I added our traditional holiday recipes in the back of Papa Dick's book and the girls are in the process of writing down three or four of their own original or most-used recipes, along with their three women cousins. This will be called *The Cousin's Cookbook*. They will then have a combined selection of recipes that will have the advantage of seven creative minds. I'm sure the pages will turn when planning a special meal or when they're stuck on dead center about what to fix for dinner.

CHAPTER *Three*
PAPA AND HIS GRANDCHILDREN

Children spell love t-i-m-e.

— OVERHEARD BY AUTHOR

The value and importance of a grandparent's time, born so many years ago for Papa Dick at the Flambeau, now flourishes with nine very receptive grandchildren.

Our ninth grandchild is Milo, a young boy born in Guatemala who has found his forever home with Meg and David. We've had plenty of experience welcoming new grandchildren into the clan, beginning with the birth of Mike.

Meg and I were doing a workshop together the evening that Mike's mother Molly went into labor. We drove into our garage that evening, anxious and excited for news. As the car headlights shone on the back of the garage we saw what Papa Dick had spray painted on the wall: "Boy! All's Well!"

In time, the inside of our garage became resplendent with spray painted colors announcing each birth.

We've also had plenty of time to think about our role as grandparents. We see ourselves as putting the frosting on the cake. If, as parents, we didn't fully understand the passage of time, we can now re-evaluate what's really important. If, as parents, we didn't understand the choices that were ours to make, we can now make more joyful choices, more often.

One of the things that both Papa Dick and I came to realize is how much pleasure there is in creating fun for those we love. I'm not sure about the adage that says playing with children will keep you younger, for we fall into bed exhausted after a day with our young family members. What I do know is that having these children in our lives has made us both creative in new ways that have brought pleasure to all of us–both the young and old.

Papa's Boot Camp

When we planned to have our six-year-old grandson Sam and his three-year-old sister Rose stay at our home for a brief three-day visit, we talked about what we might do with them during that time. Sam is a vibrant and active boy and we felt, in an effort to salvage our own energy, that having some planned activities with them would be a very good idea.

The week before the children were to arrive, Papa Dick wrote the following letter to Sam. The letter was read by both of Sam's parents, David and Meg, and then read aloud to Sam. Four times.

January 13,1998

Subject: Boot Camp

Hi Sam,

I am writing to you about your attending my boot camp.

When a young man or woman goes into the military from a civilian background, they have no experience or understanding of what it means to be a soldier. The very first day they arrive at the Army Post, they all assemble and stand in line to be addressed by the First Sergeant. He explains to them the learning process of being changed from a raw recruit to a highly trained soldier. They begin the process by going through Boot Camp.

It always begins by shaving their heads, throwing away their old and inappropriate clothing, donning proper uniforms, and learning right at the beginning to say "Yes Sir" and "No Sir." Usually, they don't catch on right

The daughters: Molly, Anne, Katie, and Meg

The Fleming Tribe

Milo

Boot Camp: Mike, Kal, Ned, Will and Sam

Lucy, Grace, and Rose

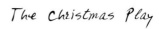

The Christmas Play

Papa Dick on the Fourth of July

The Pontoon Float

The Revolutionary Band

Sam and Ned

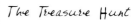
The Treasure Hunt

Ethel's Fairy House

The Bride

Granny and Granddaughters

The Cousins at the lake

Kenny and Papa Dick

Mike

Mike's Letter
Age 8

Lucy

Hi this is Mike.
Taeck you for the
Tertel Shell.
I cant whaetan
Till I can go
To the Swop
agen!

*away but the Boot Camp instructor has a way of helping
them along. When Boot Camp is over, most of the persons
have survived and from that point forward they are
stronger and better persons. They have learned to work as
a team, to be respectful of their leaders, to help their fellow soldiers such as Rose and Lucy (Sam's sisters), to be
honest and straight forward in all their actions, to be
self-reliant and to accept and carry out orders without
question or argument. I've already been through this
experience and you can see how it has helped me! In fact,
I am authorized by my own military experience to conduct Boot Camp for persons such as you.*

*It is important to understand that this is a demand-
ing and sometimes painful process, but always the final
result is that a person does become a true soldier—one
who can be counted on when the chips are down. As a
matter of fact, I have already secured an appropriate
uniform for you to wear. I plan to work directly with
you as your First Sergeant. We will leave Lucy and Rose
to be observers as they will not participate as Grunts, a
term often used to identify the person being trained.*

*I'm not sure it will be necessary to shave your head,
but in the interest of the very best final result, and with
the hope of graduating at the top of your class, it might
be best if we did that. After a few months the hair grows
back—mostly.*

*I haven't put the training course in its final form yet,
but I have made progress. I do expect that we will have a
forced march, we may do some rifle training, and we are
going to come down hard on the matter of discipline. This
is essential because when a soldier gets in a tough spot
under combat conditions survival often depends upon
instant understanding and carrying out of orders. You
have some work to do in this area and I can help you. In
that respect, it would be wise to practice some push-ups.
Your father can, I think, demonstrate how they are done.*

*I'll be thinking more about this and you should be
thinking as well. If you think of a good idea, you might*

write me a note in which you offer some of your own views. Have you ever peeled potatoes? Have you ever scrubbed a floor? Hauled firewood? Washed dirty pots and pans? These are just some aspects of Boot Camp. Of course, it is not all long hours and miserable work and carrying out orders. When a Grunt has successfully completed Boot Camp there is a celebration and possible rewards for those who have distinguished themselves!

With deep anticipation and love even deeper,

Your First Sergeant

It should be noted that Sam's father David had probably not done a push-up since physical education class in high school and then only under distress. It should further be noted that Papa Dick is not a sterling example of how Boot Camp helped him.

Following the reading of the letter to Sam, the following remarks were heard:

"Papa was just kidding about the haircut wasn't he?" (Sam has a mass of dark curls).

"What about the rifle training?" Although there are no guns in Sam's home, his parents have talked to him several times about the danger of firearms. It was agreed that since Papa Dick is a duck hunter, it just might be a good idea to learn about handling guns from someone Sam respects and looks up to. They knew the emphasis would be on gun safety.

It was agreed. Sam would be Papa Dick's first recruit. The day arrived for Sam and Rose to come for their visit and no one was expecting what happened next. As soon as Sam saw Papa, he saluted, fell to the floor and did some push-ups. He did these things before he said hello or gave us a hug. Papa Dick, amused with his idea, had been shopping before the visit and presented Sam with bib overalls and a long sleeved T-shirt in a camouflage pattern with olive green and brown oak leafs. Sam received his uniform with a mixture of pleasure and guarded suspicion. What was coming next? The first evening was spent storytelling with Papa Dick relating some remembrances from his own basic training in the Army.

Sam—First Day of Boot Camp

The following morning the much anticipated rifle appeared in the crook of Papa's arm. The kitchen table was cleared and an old wool blanket placed on top of the table. On the blanket was a yellow legal pad and pencil. Itchy fingers longed to hold the unloaded rifle but first came instructions from the First Sergeant. Papa Dick looked intently at the big brown eyes staring back at him. "I'm going to tell you something that you must memorize and never forget." The black curls nodded once with total acceptance.

"Never point a gun at any living creature unless you mean to kill it. If you forget this rule and point a gun at any living thing, our lesson will be over immediately. I will not get mad at you or raise my voice. I will simply put the rifle away and bring it out again when you are older. Do you understand?"

There was another swift head nod.

"Tell me the most important rule." Sam repeated the rule. "Another important rule is, if you ever see a gun in someone else's home, don't touch it. Tell an adult right away where the gun is. Do you know why this is so important?"

"My dad told me this. He said I would never know if the gun was loaded."

"Excellent, Sam! All guns that you touch are regarded as loaded until you have personally and safely inspected them to prove to yourself they are not loaded. Therefore, you handle the gun as if it were loaded."

Papa Dick drew the workings of a gun on the yellow pad. Questions were asked and answered. Sam then learned how to carry a gun. Papa Dick demonstrated and then Sam was told to pick up the rifle and to do so according to what was discussed and demonstrated. Sam so very carefully picked up the rifle, pointing the muzzle safely to the floor and inspected it to prove it was not loaded. So far, so good.

It was now time to go outside to a pre-arranged target site. If ever a young boy could be allowed, in the midst of his excitement, to have a lapse of memory, surely this was that time. "Sam, you carry the gun," Papa Dick directed.

One of Papa Dick's rewards that morning was watching Sam pick up the unloaded rifle and carry it just the way he was taught. We live in the country and the target area was in a clump of trees where a plastic bottle filled with red dye had been placed on a stump. Dick taught Sam to position the unloaded rifle on his ATV for a firm siting place. A single bullet was put in the chamber. Sam was given the first shot and, wonder of wonders, scored a direct hit with the red water bottle bursting causing large splatters of red to stain the snow. Sam was speechless. So was Papa Dick.

The rules were discussed again and more practice followed. It was a memorable morning.

We have four other grandsons and the word is out. Sam called Kal, Kal called Mike and Mike told Ned and Will. "Papa is a First Sergeant and he's having Boot Camp for us at the cottage this summer!"

The challenge for Papa Dick now became what to include in the summer Boot Camp. Never at a loss for free advice or suggestions, other family members gave their input. It soon became clear that the final choices would be Papa's. His first decision was to give himself a promotion. Papa Dick is now the Commanding Officer and Gene and David, as his sons-in-law, are First Sergeants.

Boot Camp has evolved with an ever greater emphasis on personal responsibility, self reliance, knowledge and adventure. Such activities as forest lore, the use of a compass and map reading, identification of animals, birds, trees and plants, cooking out of doors, building a tree house and star gazing have been added to the basic skills.

Our friends who are aware of Boot Camp have asked Papa Dick if he would accept their young grandsons on a tuition basis, but not everyone is so enthusiastic. Papa's three granddaughters have informed him that they are not interested. Lucy suggested that a great idea for the boys would be to take them deep in the woods, *ala* Hansel and Gretel, and tell them to find their own way back to the cottage. This activity, in her opinion, would then allow for some uninterrupted dress up time for the girls without jeers or mockery from the boys, who were after all, being SHAPED UP! As time has passed, the girls have become interested in some of the adventures and have joined in. The uniforms the boys wear, however, have been totally rejected.

Over the Fourth of July family get together, Papa Dick, Gene and David planned a bivouac and invited our fourteen-year-old nephew Frank and his father Mike to join in. That made six Grunts and four Officers. Tents were set up and food was bought for both an evening and breakfast meal. Both meals were to be cooked over an open fire pit. The Grunts did the work, gathering firewood, digging the fire pit, pitching the tents and each boy had clean-up chores. Ned, one of the Grunts, was in charge of the American flag that was attached to a birch pole. The care and respect for the flag was solemnly discussed by an officer. Squirt guns were handed out to the delight of the Grunts. One of the Officers explained that anyone who did not obey the rules or fulfill their assignments would go up against a squirt gun firing squad. As an example, Papa Dick was tied to a tree, blindfolded and asked if he had any last words. He replied, "Strawberry Shortcake!" First Sergeant David then formed the firing squad and following the commands, "Ready! Aim! Fire!", Papa was drenched with water amid whoops and peals of laughter.

The adventure continued. Together, the troop explored a beaver lodge during a forced march. A deep woods search located an artesian well. Teams of two boys in canoes played "Capture the Flag." Three orange flags had been placed in different locations on the lake. All the Grunts shook hands after the event just as they have witnessed sports stars doing following a competition. They took a night hike and Papa read *The Cremation of Sam*

Anne and Steven

McGee, one of Robert Service's poems, as they sat around the campfire before lights out.

During Labor Day weekend, when we were all together, Anne's husband Steven, an Astro Physicist with NASA, was asked to give the Grunts and any other interested family members information on the Universe including Black Holes, theories of life on other planets, and his own research on ice particles and the existence of outer space forms of life. Everyone was interested, along with some other families on the lake. Steven had his workshop after dark in a clearing where the night sky was clearly visible. Sitting on blankets on the grass, everyone formed a circle around Steven. What an opportunity for the adults and the children to learn and to ask questions from someone who was so knowledgeable. As Steven spoke in his soft Scottish brogue, younger children fell asleep on their parent's laps while the older children and adults remained transfixed.

The next planned Boot Camp experience will be building a treehouse this summer. The Grunts will design, plan and build this retreat. Location, logistics and architecture are still under discussion.

I don't know what lies ahead for Boot Camp but the enthusiasm from both the Grunts and Officers remains high. As the children grow older, fishing and canoe trips exploring surrounding lakes and rivers, more bivouacs, trips to Lake Superior and continued outdoor cooking skills are high on the list of proposed adventures. I know that our granddaughters will join in on many of these forays into the lakes and woods because they have the same love of the out-of-doors, the passion for adventure and the curiosity and courage to risk a new experience. Some memorable adventures have already happened in our family and valuable character traits have been reinforced because of Papa's Boot Camp.

Letters

Conversations between a grandparent and grandchild are often precious and sometimes are told and retold to anyone with the patience and interest to listen. Letter writing is a way to bridge the gap between those who cannot have the face to face contact they might desire. Although e-mail is becoming an increasingly popular way for grandparents to communicate with their offspring, old-fashioned letter writing still has the advantage of being a way to create a permanent record of special relationships. And, besides that, every child loves to get mail addressed just to them.

Several years ago, Papa Dick initiated the idea of exchanging letters with our then eleven-year-old granddaughter Lucy, who was born visually impaired and uses a Braille writer and printer. The idea behind these letters, as you'll soon see, was more than just an exchange of current news. These letters would give the writers a chance to explore philosophical ideas with each other.

Papa Dick opened the dialogue by writing:

Dear Lucy,

I'm just so glad to be your Papa Dick. Some days when I am maybe a little discouraged, I think of your wonderful attack on life and the joy you take and give and it makes me stronger. We all need to know some persons like that and you are in my inner circle.

I have an idea. You can think about it, but I would like a response. My idea is that we identify a subject of interest to each of us, one that we might approach as a mystery or maybe one in which we may presume that we will have differing points of view–like hunting ducks!

When we agree on the subject, you will write your notions to me and I'll respond with my ideas. This would not really be a debate, but instead an opportunity to learn together and, I think, a good use of our time. As an example, I would be interested in hearing your views about HOW TO LIVE A LIFE THAT IS WELL-LIVED. This is only an example and, if you are game, you pick a subject of interest to you.

Well, how about it? I'd love to exchange some correspondence with you. In the years ahead these exchanges could become known as the "Papa and Lucy letters".

Love, Papa Dick

Lucy wrote back :

Dear Papa Dick,

I think that conversing through letters is a great idea. I also think the topic of "how to live a well lived life" is a very good one. What do you think? It is a very mysterious subject. I think about it a lot. The play I'm in is going well, I have eight more rehearsals. I like getting letters, especially if the letters discuss matters of interest. I think this will be fun. Please write soon.

Love, Lucy

P.S. One important thing about living a life well lived is to always notice your feelings and surroundings. Me

Dear Lucy,

I was interested to learn from your letter you think about how to lead a good life a lot. That very fact confirms that this is a good subject for us to explore further for I, too, think about it a lot. The PS you added says "one important thing about leading a good life is to always notice your feelings and surroundings." That is a very astute observation. I completely agree with that view. I think another important thing to support a good life is to love a few persons and know that they love you, too.

This morning I noticed motion from the bathroom window and after peering closely I spotted a wild turkey in the pine trees. It jumped to the ground and started looking for food—acorns, I think. What a beautiful bird!

I'm eager for your next letter.

Love, Papa Dick

Dear Papa Dick,

I think to live a good life people should use their imagination more. I use my imagination when I'm bored, and then I'm not bored anymore. I also use it when I'm doing something I don't want to do. For example, when I clean my room when I really want to read. I play an imaginary game.

The play is going good. I got a new part in it. I sing a solo.

Love, Lucy

Dear Lucy,

I really enjoy your letters. You express yourself beautifully!

I'm interested and curious about where you are going with your life. Someone-maybe Yogi Berra-said, "If you don't know where you are going, you aren't likely to get there".

Here is an idea. Could you tell me what your life situation would be like five years into the future, if everything was turning out in a way that would really satisfy you? You will be sixteen years old in five years. Then, how about when you are 25 years old and, finally, when you are Nana Joan's age and, my goodness, she is 65 years old.

Nobody can see clearly what the future holds, but that is not the question. The question is: What do you see for your life situation at those intervals if everything turns out the way you would like it to be?

I'll read your reply very carefully. Then, I'll send back a similar "look ahead" for my own life in the years to come.

Love, Papa Dick

Dear Papa Dick,

When I'm sixteen, I want to be much further along in piano, guitar and accordion.

I want to have read all of the Newberry Award winning books. And all of the Madeleine l'Engle books. I want to become better on the potter's wheel. I want to be in more plays. And begin taking voice lessons. I want to be a good babysitter. I want to be a better sailor, kayaker, rower, and canoer (even though I don't think the last three are words!). I want to be on toe shoes for ballet. I want to get a guide dog because I like dogs and think a guide would help me alot. I want to be fluent in Spanish, Italian, Latin, Greek, German and the language of the Dakota Native American tribe. And I want to be a better tap dancer. I also want to be an excellent swimmer. I want to be a published writer, but that's an all-time goal. The sooner the better!

When I'm 25, I want to have gone to college and done the Peace Corps. I want to be an anthropologist, actress, singer, dancer and writer. I'm going to work, when I'm younger, at the Red Balloon Bookstore. I like to go there and consult people about what books they might like to buy. All the workers say I'm a big help. I think I would like to live in Bayfield, Duluth or Marine on St. Croix. I want to become a mother sometime around when I'm 25. I don't know if I want to adopt a child or have a child of my own.

When I'm 65, (this is definitely the hardest) I want to be a grandmother. I want to be an accomplished anthropologist. I would like to do something like what Elizabeth Cady Stanton and Susan B. Anthony were able to do for Wymyn's Rights.

If I think of anything else, I'll send you another letter.

Love, Lucy

Dear Lucy,

I just re-read your reply to how you see your life. You are attacking life on a broad front and, in that process, you continue to reveal commitment to be helpful to others. That is just outstanding.

Well, I promised to tell you some of my views as to what my life will be like in the years ahead. My time frame will be more compressed than yours. My first and deepest wish is that Joan will be close by. I cannot conceive of daily existence without her presence. At 70 years of age, I want to be living with a daily purpose. I want to keep an active list of things that need to be done by me. I want to be present and play with family and keep close track of the growing up process and be a part of it. I'd like to find a way to use my career experience and beliefs in the building of solid life insurance agents. I'd like to strengthen just a few people.

Shoot, Lucy, I want all of these things each and every day for all the days that are left to me. I can't narrow this to certain intervals. I can see that some more thinking on this is necessary. You have already been helpful to me so I propose we do more of that. What do you say?

Love, Papa Dick

Goalsetting With Grandchildren

I often wonder how I could have lived so many years without becoming an active goalsetter. Since learning the process, it's had an enormous, positive impact on my life. My editor Barbara Winter says, "When you're consciously setting goals, your life becomes filled with recognizable coincidences." Her exciting life reflects her philosophy.

It's important to me to do things that will enlarge our grandchildren's view of themselves and the world they live in. Their parents believe so strongly in this concept that it is wonderful for me to find a way to support their actions with their children. We agree that we never want the children to undervalue themselves or be afraid to dream big dreams.

I started a dialogue with grandson Mike just as he began his first year as a teenager. I remembered reading in Richard Leider's newsletter *On Purpose* about John Goddard and his list of one hundred and twenty-seven lifetime goals, written when he was fifteen years old. Goddard's philosophy was, "*To dare is to do. To fear is to fail.*" A generation after writing his list, he had accomplished one hundred and eighteen of his quests.

I talked to Mike about John Goddard. He was amazed and, I believe, intrigued when, out of his own awareness, his eyes were open to the possibilities that might exist for him. To further prime the pump, I told Mike about some goals I have. My Goals List included:

Kayak on Lake Superior.

Learn to speak some German and plan a trip with Papa Dick to Germany.

Explore Steven's Scotland places he loves and Anne has come to love. Visit his family and friends.

To return to weekly yoga exercises.

To read everything Isak Dinesen wrote.

To plan a workshop with Lucy exploring how to live with greater abundance.

To write another book continuing my thoughts in my booklet ZESTFUL WOMEN!

To be on a talk show on grandparenting.

To attend an Andrea Bocelli concert or opera with everyone in our family.

To make dumplings and egg noodles the way my mother made them.

To travel on the Orient Express in Europe. Will I need a veiled hat?

To my astonishment and pride, a few weeks later Mike gave me his list:

Visit Australia.

Invent something helpful.

Create a computer game.

Catch a sixteen-inch bass.

Discover a new animal.

Climb a mountain.

Ride a hot air balloon over the Caribbean.

Scuba dive in a freshwater lake.

See a cell divide.

Enter and finish the Eco-Challenge.

Write a book.

Explore a rainforest.

Climb a tree and see the canopy of a rainforest.

Find a cure for cancer.

Create a name page on the Internet.

Paddle down a river in a canoe.

Create, plan and draw the tide.

Build a go-cart.

Draw and paint a beautiful picture.

Go on a camping trip deep in the woods. (Boot Camp 2000)

Stay on an island and record what I see.

Get straight A's one whole year on my report card.

Hike ten miles.

The Fleming Family Theater Troupe

Our family plays had a promising start when Papa Dick agreed, with little reluctance, to participate. We started, simply enough, by acting out a favorite children's book. The guiding force was our then eight-year-old granddaughter Lucy's interest in books, plays and dressing up.

Our first entry into the world of theater was in our living room, with three main actors. Our script was the book *Strega Nona*, which means grandmother witch. I played the witch. Lucy was the little granddaughter and Papa Dick played Big Anthony, a lovable, but bumbling, fellow. I read from the book as we all acted out our parts. Our black lab Traveler did reasonably well playing a goat. I wore a scarf, representing a babushka, with a colorful shawl. Lucy wore a poncho and petticoat found in a trunk of play clothes. Papa Dick wore a slouch hat and an old fishing jacket.

Our props were a big kettle representing the pasta pot, a large wooden spoon and a mound of pillows suggesting the mountains. We had four dress rehearsals until Lucy was satisfied that Papa Dick understood his part. Since I had the script, she wasn't as demanding of me. We all thought it was a lovely way to spend an evening.

One Thanksgiving the grandchildren all acted out an original play written by Dr. Leuss (Lucy) called *The Grumpy Grinch's Thanksgiving*. Lucy's mother Meg put up two bed sheets for a curtain and all the mothers helped find a few costumes and props. Lucy's younger brother Sam had reached the limit of his endurance as far as taking orders from his older sister. In the middle of the play he started eating a cookie. A frustrated Lucy insisted he'd missed his cue and Sam said he'd say his line as soon as he finished his cookie. He proceeded to take infinitesimal bites and then chew them as slowly as possible.

Christmas was coming and early in December Lucy called to say that she had written her own version of the Christmas story and had given everyone in the family a role, casting herself as the Virgin Mary. She ran out of roles for the adults so she added two additional characters: Aunt Molly would be the midwife, a role she felt was overlooked, and I would play the part of the Virgin Mary's mother. Surely Jesus had grandparents!

Lucy's offering was met with mixed feelings from the five little boys, ranging from mild interest to stubborn refusal. Will, who was five at the time, wanted nothing to do with a play. It was Papa Dick's willing participation and enthusiasm that turned the tide–for everyone but Will. Papa Dick made a manger out of wood and filled it with handfuls of straw that was covering his garden. He accepted the role of Joseph and wore one of his old bathrobes. His acting was appropriately sober and serious.

Three of the boys then agreed to their roles and were even more enticed when they learned they would carry sticks (staffs), wear paper crowns decorated with fake jewels along with a velvet vest, colorful tunic and a blouse with gold threading borrowed from Grandmother's closet. One was to carry a jewelry box filled with chocolate wrapped in gold foil to look like coins, the second carried a perfume bottle and the third a painted wooden box, their gifts for the baby.

Grace and Rose were then two years old and they wore beautiful gold wings that Meg made. They each had one line. Rose was to say, "A baby is born," and Grace was to say, "and he is Christ the Lord." They were coached without mercy by their mothers. After realizing, during dress rehearsal, that they were getting the lion's share of attention, they spoke their one line again and again with no regard for the script.

You may remember that Lucy was the author, director, organ player for the hymns sung before, during and after the production *and* the Virgin Mary. The stress was building!

Aunt Kate was the prompter. Her role took on an even greater significance as she went from child to child whispering the forgotten lines, directing their movements, or trying to keep a lid on their mischief and lack of proper respect for their director. During the dress rehearsals, Will was peeking through downcast eyes. His moment of truth came. Was there a part for him? Papa Dick grabbed a star from the Christmas tree and told him that he was Star Man. It was his star that the wise men would see in the sky. He did an admirable job, holding the star in an upraised position without ever resting his arm.

After several tense rehearsals, the play started. For a few brief moments it was silent night. Suddenly Lucy called a halt. With a shriek of despair she said the doll (Jesus) should have been under her blue robe, not laying in the manger because "He wasn't even born yet!" The play started again with the baby in its proper place. Molly the midwife told her how to swaddle the baby following its birth.

All went well until the Virgin Mary (Lucy) walked over to the old pump organ and began to belt out *Angels We Have Heard on High*. Since not everyone in our family can carry a tune, since the old organ had not been tuned for seventy years, since Papa Dick has trouble hearing and doesn't have his hearing aids turned on very high when all the grandchildren are around, the result was not good. After a few chords, Lucy cried "Stop!" Some kept singing, having missed the directive. Reminding several of us of the Phantom in *Phantom of the Opera*, she banged one final chord and turned around facing us. "When I say stop, I mean STOP!" she commanded. She turned some of us to stone.

We took it from the top and this time managed to complete the play before anyone starved to death. Relief, cheers and congratulations all the way around followed the performance.

Most children's books can easily be adapted to a family play and there are two that we're thinking about for future Christmas's: *The Story of Holly and Ivy* by Rumer Godden and *The Christmas Mouse* by Elisabeth Wenning.

Holly and Ivy is a story of an orphan girl and a Christmas doll in a toy store who also yearns for a home of her own and someone to love her. The cast includes Ivy, Holly, a policeman and his wife, the owner of the toy store, a young boy who works there and a few talking stuffed animals. The props could include a small Christmas tree, a pile of blankets that Ivy falls asleep on, a table setting for breakfast, and the doll Holly—all easily assembled items.

The Christmas Mouse is the story of Casper Kleinmouse, a church mouse in Austria. When Casper, who was born in the church one Christmas, becomes very hungry, he eats the bellows inside the church organ, causing the organist Franz Gruber great upset because there will be no music for midnight mass. The pastor Father Mohr resists setting mousetraps because he had first seen Casper asleep in the crèche and named him. It is Father Mohr who wrote the words and Franz Gruber the music to a new Christmas song. Together they sang *Silent Night* in that little church in Oberndorf, Austria. The cast includes Casper, Father Mohr, Mr. Gruber, his wife, and members of the church choir. The props might include a crèche, cookies (Mrs. Gruber is baking), a guitar and a piano or something representing the organ and the music for *Silent Night*. I'd suggest having a camera at hand and food available when the play is over.

The Script for the Thanksgiving Play

The Grumpy Grinches Thanksgiving by Dr. Leuss (Lucy)

Cast: Grinch—Mike
    Cindy Lou Who—Lucy
    You Who—Ned
    Boo Who—Will
    Max—Sam

Act I : Wherein the Grinch demonstrates he does not know how to say "thank you."

Scene I: Grinch and Max in Grinches cave.

Grinch— I hate Thanksgiving!
    Giving thanks is a sham.
    I'd rather just eat who-pudding and some ham.

    Giving thanks stinks.
    That's what me-thinks.
    Just give me some spuds and a lamb.

Scene II: Enter Cindy Lou Who (a knock is heard at the front door)

Cindy Lou Who—

    Hello Grinch. I'm Cindy Lou Who.
    And I'm not more than two.

    Did I hear you say you don't like to say thank you?
    Well, my mom always says,
    Come rain or shine,
    You've got to say thank you
    All of the time.

Max— Even I can say thank you
    With a wag of my tail.
    You don't hear me grousing,
    With a whine and a wail.

Cindy Lou Who—

> You Who and Boo Who will know what to do
> I better go get them, so we can teach you
> To give proper thanks
> And stop your evil, grinchy pranks.

Act II: Wherein the no's have invited the Grinch for Thanksgiving dinner to show him how they say thank you.

Scene I: Who's dinner table.

You Who—We've invited the Grinch to our Thanksgiving feast.
> We're going to have hash and rare Who roast beast.

Boo Who—Welcome, our friend. We're glad that you are here. It's better than Christmas when Max was a reindeer.

Cindy Lou Who—

> (center stage)
> We're here to give thanks for the trees and the flowers
> We're here to give thanks for the days and the hours
> We spend with our family and our very best friends.
> We're here to give thanks to our dear Mother Earth
> We're here to give thanks from the time of our birth
> To the planet that gives us our food and our home.

Scene Two:

> Grinches response (center stage)

Grinch— I'm glad to be part of the Who family
> I've found that it's fun to say thank you. You see?

All (rising)

> And what happened then?
> Well in Whoville we say
> that the Grinches small heart
> grew three sizes that day!
>
> And the minute his heart
> didn't feel quite so tight
> His mouth opened up and said "thank you."
> That's right!

Kenny at the River with Mike and Papa Dick

How do the generations in a family come to know each other? One way this can happen is to take your grandchild to a place that has special meaning for you and spend some one-on-one time talking about an interest you are eager to share with them. Papa Dick chose the Mississippi River for such an outing with grandson Mike.

Papa Dick is a duck hunter and has for years had a shack, built with five other friends, in Buffalo City, Wisconsin. Several years ago, Dick met Kenny Salwey, an authentic man of the river. Kenny is most at home along or on the river, in the woods or in his one room shack on the river's edge. He is a hunter and trapper, an environmentalist, a poet and philosopher. Kenny is a lover of dogs and critters, as he calls them, and is a sentimental and tender man. He is also a member of the Slow Talkers of America.

For many years he has combined his interest in children and young adults with his passion about the area of the country where he lives. He is a master storyteller and no matter how slow he may be talking, his audiences in schoolrooms and nature reserves are captivated. Some years ago, Papa Dick and Kenny sat down with a tape recorder between them and Kenny told some of his stories while Papa Dick encouraged him by asking questions. Papa Dick wanted to do this to preserve the stories for his young grandchildren. Since both men can really spin a yarn, the tapes are delightful.

When Mike was eight, Papa Dick decided that he and Kenny would introduce him to the river and swampland areas, encouraging Mike to discover for himself the reverence and love of nature they both have. The deal was made and the day came. One spring day, dressed much like Papa Dick, in a flannel shirt and canvas pants with high rubber boots, Mike left with his grandfather. An inexpensive camera was slung around his neck and explorer's hats completed their outfits. That day might well have helped forge Mike's future. It certainly instilled in him the developing values of appreciation for nature and knowledge of animals as seen through Kenny's eyes.

He saw in Kenny a man who had chosen not to be confined to the spaces and expectations of others and that appealed to Mike. Imagine having a career that was mostly spent out of doors! Kenny also talked about how important reading and education are in preparation for a life of your own choosing. I don't find it a coincidence that in the last four years Mike has become an avid reader, excellent student and now talks about a career in the Australian outback.

When Mike returned home he started decorating his small playhouse with the treasures he had found or Kenny had given him. Turtle shells, a raccoon tail, feathers and beaver teeth now adorn his room. Not surprisingly, Mike's playhouse bears some resemblance to Kenny's shack.

Kenny's shack consists of a single room with bunks along one side. The walls are filled with all manner of interesting things: some cookware, skulls, pelts, pictures, hornet nests, favorite sayings, dried plants and herbs and notes from children who have heard him speak. A small wood stove, necessary kindling, table and chairs and many books make it a magical place. It's a place of peace and quiet, a place to palaver, as Kenny would say, a place to read and think about what's really important in one's life.

As the three of them were standing near the shack and looking out at the river, Kenny told them a story about two wild Canadian geese that came back year after year. Kenny named them Big Boy and Beauty. Every spring their return was greeted by Kenny and through the years he watched them raise their young until autumn came and they migrated with a flock to a warmer climate. Kenny is a trapper and some of his traps were in the vicinity of the nesting geese. One day the unexpected happened and Big Boy caught one webbed foot in a trap. By the time Kenny realized what was happening, Big Boy was frantically swimming under water in a futile attempt to rid himself of this dreadful object. A distraught Beauty was honking and flying in circles over the roiled water. Jumping in his canoe, Kenny started the grand chase to free Big Boy. When he was within inches of the big bird, Big Boy would lunge forward or dive under the water. Beauty never gave up her honking vigil in the sky above the remarkable drama below.

After a time, when Big Boy was utterly exhausted and probably near death, Kenny reached down and freed him. The last vision Kenny had of the pair of geese that day was seeing them together on a mud flat—a drake and his mate with her protective wing around his haggard body. Geese mate for life.

I, too, spent a day in the swamp with Kenny and Papa Dick. We were walking and visiting when Kenny pointed out the remains of a huge tree trunk. Kenny told us that the tree had saved his life one late fall when an early winter storm had struck without warning. With lightning flashing, rain, snow and hail swirling, Kenny wisely crawled into the hollow trunk of the tree with his black lab Joey and spent the night. I crawled into the hollow and took a small piece of the tree to add to my spiritual collection of things found in the woods.

Papa Dick is planning a Boot Camp adventure for his five grandsons that will include meeting Kenny to experience the swamp before spending the evening at the duck shack. Knowing a free-thinker like Kenny is another way of showing our grandchildren that this big world contains many different ways of living.

The Treasure Hunt

I'm not sure what motivated Papa Dick to plan a treasure hunt. It may have been a long ago reading of *Treasure Island* or maybe an awareness of an older grandson's interest in Native American culture or perhaps just the fun of it all was the main motivation. Where to begin?

The location would be somewhere on the shore of a Wisconsin lake where we have a summer cottage. A treasure hunt needs a map, preferably one that's passed through many hands. We found an old chamois cloth hanging on a hook in the garage, complete with a few well-worn holes and no markings to date it. I went to the library and found books on Native American symbols including a symbol for treasure. Papa Dick drew a crude drawing of the lake and added things like where the loons nest, the big beaver lodge and the eagle's nest, high on a white pine tree. The symbol we found for treasure was a box with rays coming from it which he added to the map along with four canoes with the treasure box on the lake. He drew a sun and moon indicating directions and other clues that were difficult, but accurate.

When we were together on Thanksgiving, he told the older children that he heard of an old woodcutter who lived in the area who had in his possession a very old treasure map. Did the children want to see if Papa Dick could get it? "Yes, of course," they shouted.

Later Papa Dick reported that he had contacted Tony Gill, the woodcutter, and he agreed to let the grandchildren search for the treasure. The excitement was building and their curiosity was intense. The children got the map and were told that the hunt would be held over the Fourth of July when we'd be together at the cottage. Meanwhile the three families would take turns being the keeper of the map and they were encouraged to show it to their friends and take it to their classrooms. Excitement was mounting! Who would be the one to discover the treasure's location?

Meanwhile, Papa Dick and I were gathering artifacts that just might appear in a real buried treasure. I found a wonderful ancient box with leather straps. The straps were moldy and one was broken. We found some old clay beads, a basket woven from sweet grass and a handmade hatchet that we stuck a few feathers on. About this time, we learned about a young couple that lived in a log cabin in the woods about forty miles from our home who make replicas of Native American tools and musical pieces to sell at art fairs during the summer months. In their garage Papa Dick found a jaw bone painted with symbols, a battered case that included everything they needed to start a fire, stones with paintings on them, eagle feathers and a marvelous well-worn doll called a grandmother doll. This doll had been used to teach two generations of young girls how to make deer hide clothes and do decorative beadwork. All of these interesting objects were added to the treasure chest.

The day of the treasure hunt arrived. The evening before Papa Dick, Gene and David had received permission from another landowner to bury the box on their property. The men dug a hole about two feet deep, inserted the treasure and then covered the raw earth with leaves and moss. Papa had found a six inch pyramid-shaped rock and that was placed on top of the buried box.

The treasure was buried about twenty feet from another clue, the rotted and weathered remains of an old rowboat.

The following morning we gathered in our pontoon boat. With the map spread out between the older boys and their absorbed heads again checking the clues to convince themselves that they had figured it out, Papa steered the boat in the direction they gave him. The day was cool and overcast with a lack of wind and stillness that somehow seemed ominous. Mike whispered that we should have called *National Geographic* to take photos.

We arrived at the correct site with Mike, Ned and Kal intently scanning the shoreline. Lucy sat very quietly in deep concentration. She told me later that she was wishing there would be an Indian doll among the treasure. Dick brought a long steel probe and told the children that if they found any clues or thought we should dig in a certain place, he would probe the ground and if we heard a thump we'd dig. For about a half hour the search went on. Wild, excited children ran around and a few probes that bore no treasure were abandoned. Suddenly, the pyramid rock was discovered. Mike asked his father to probe around the rock that could be the final clue. A circle of children and adults quickly surrounded the area and when we heard the thump, we knew that something lay under the ground. Lucy knelt down and felt the progress as the digging cautiously began. The top of the old box was uncovered and Papa announced, "Well, there's clearly something here!"

I hesitate to tell you what happened next because it may sound like I'm taking poetic license to make a good story even better. Yet, it did happen. The day that was so quiet suddenly changed as a wind materialized scattering last autumn's oak leaves in spirals. The children exchanged guarded glances–fear or a hesitancy to dig further perhaps? And then the whispered word, "Spirits!"

The excitement, however, did not prevent them from looking inside the box. They did and Sam, fully aware of his sister's love for dolls, grabbed the three dolls which were handed over to a triumphant Lucy. She, in turn, reluctantly presented both Rose and Grace with one, fearful that they were not old enough to take proper care of them. The five boys dove for the jawbone and hatchet. Everything the box contained was examined with great interest.

The box, along with its treasures, has found its home at our cottage since the children believe that because of the spirits, nothing should be disturbed. This is not completely true since the dolls live with their adopted mothers.

The children take the box out of the closet now and again, either to show friends, to examine the contents again or to speculate, "Is there more treasure on Little Sissabagama?"

Kal's Report on The Treasure Hunt

The fun and excitement. From what I know began when my grandma, Joan Fleming got a treasure map from a very nice man. If your thinking this story can't be real because the woodcutter would have kept it or sold to a museum. This man hadn't much of a family…he had no kids to share the excitement with. I haven't met the nice man yet and know who he was but if he ever reads this my hole family thanks you. When we all got together (meaning the family) grandma showed it to us all. We stared and listened to her story then we all tried to figure it out. We hadn't found where the treasure map was but we had one clue: it was on our lake, lake Sissabagama. Finely after a couple months we got together again and about 3 times before that but we didn't get any clues those last three times. When we got together this last time (hopefully) Uncle Gene had an idea (drawing of a light bulb) he showed it to us all. We all gave it a look and agreed it did look like it made an X. We set off to see if. he was right and of course on the way there Aunt Molly, Aunt Meg and my Mom had to take a million pictures. We docked upon the shore and jumped off to tie the rope so the boat wouldn't float away. I knew we would find the treasure if not here, somewhere. As we started our walk I saw two paths crossing to form an X. It had to be around there somewhere then. Later Mike found a pointed up rock. We took turns digging but I wasn't much help on that part. Uncle Gene took a stroke and it hit the box. He lifted it out and everyone dug around inside to find beads, necklesses, dolles, tools, scalp, leaders bones, and a painted on the skull of an animal. There was a snake skin, arrow heads and pouches. It was a great adventure I'd never forget.

Kal wrote his story when he was nine, although the adventure took place three years earlier. What do children remember from such an experience? I asked them.

MIKE: I was excited because I knew we were about to find it and I figured out where it was. I felt good about that! There were arrowheads, rocks and interesting artifacts in it. At the time I thought there was more to it and I figured out that there might be something more on Big Island.

NED: Me and Mike everyday would try and find out what the map meant. I remember I held an ax and there was a snake skin in a basket that some of us were afraid of. It was fun!

WILL: I was just excited cause we found the treasure! I hope there is some more around. I hope the next time we visit Grandma we might go on a treasure hunt! I'm glad cause I got to pick things and feel things that were in it. It was fun just going on a treasure hunt with all us cousins.

LUCY: I remember waiting for Tony the woodcutter to call and tell us if we could use his treasure map. I remember the pine trees rustling when the wind blew…when we found the treasure!

SAM: Happy, excited feeling when we hit the treasure box and feeling foolish when I asked Papa to use his probe and he hit a rock!

Tarps and Bungi Cords

Before we did some remodeling of our very old cottage, we had a small bedroom that was fondly called the "hell hole." No one wanted to sleep on the ancient steel bunk beds in this room because it smelled like mold. The room found its rightful place in life by our five grandsons when they decided it would make a perfect fort.

Using an odd collection of worn and torn blankets and old sheets, the boys would play for hours making their forts in every configuration imaginable. Insisting that the door remained closed until they invited the rest of us in to see their most recent creation, the room offered a bonus of relative peace and quiet while they were designing. "NO ADULTS ALLOWED" with a skull and crossbones was written and taped to the door.

The "hell hole" later became a bathroom, featuring the claw foot bathtub that belonged to Papa Dick's Great Aunt Kate. He remembers baths in the old tub that, when not in use, had a fitted, flowered cotton covering on the top. Everyone was pleased with the new bathroom except the boys. Their disappointment was appeased when Papa Dick bought a variety of tarps in different sizes and colors and an array of multicolored bungi cords. They now build their forts outside and have expanded both their imagination and their games.

An Outhouse to the Rescue

One bathroom for a cottage that sometimes swells with seventeen people, including those outside in tents, can make for some interesting "dances" even if there are those who take advantage of the great outdoors. Papa Dick decided to build an outhouse to stem the tide, so to speak.

Seldom has a building project had more curious onlookers or more willing helpers. Great attention was paid to the height and type of the toilet seat. Should the seat be wood? Should it be plastic? Hard or soft? Papa Dick made the choice: soft, the kind you can sink into. After the project was finished, a can of root beer christened the essential work of art.

Now came the real test of an outhouse: how do we get them to use it? Papa Dick decided to outsmart his grandchildren. He bought a cheap collection of stuff that kids like. He gathered them together and announced that whenever they actually used the outhouse they'd get a slip of colored paper from him. Whoever collected the most slips would be the first to pick their prize, followed by the others in descending order. It looked like there was a deer trail to the outhouse by the end of the first weekend the outhouse was in use. Ned, who was nine, was especially clever. He kept drinking glasses of water throughout the day and won first pick.

Our outhouse contains a message board and black magic marker for anyone who wants to write a message about something or a note to someone. A favorite was one written by David: *"Remember, stressed is desserts spelled backwards!"*

Miniature Log Houses

On rainy cottage days we look for things to do in front of the fireplace. On drippy days, Papa Dick encourages outside projects always claiming that "It looks worse from the inside. Once you get outside it's not so bad!" Enticing some of the boys outside on one such day, he told them they'd go into the woods, cut some small saplings and bring them back to the cottage. After removing the twigs and leaves, he cut the saplings into lengths of ten, eight, six and three inches. Then they could build miniature log houses or forts. Armed with a glue gun and supervised by Papa Dick and parents, the building project was set up. Moss was stuffed between the cracks and stones were collected for the fireplace, to be used both inside and on an outside wall of the log building and for the chimney.

One of our favorite family sayings is, "Uncle Gene could do it!" He's our resident expert and he willingly provides encouragement and direction for all building projects. After this project, it looked as if Gene would have competition since the boys took to their building with gusto. This beginning project was such a hit, that more extensive building projects are in store.

Papa Dick and Nana's Audiotapes

The idea of making audiotapes for grandchildren developed from a need. Our granddaughter Lucy was born severely visually impaired. She has a disease called Lebers Congenital Amaurosis that attacks the retina and has left her without sight. Her parents suggested that everyone in the family make an audiotape for her so she could become familiar with our voices. We bought a sixty-minute tape so that Papa Dick could fill thirty minutes and I would do the same. Our simple tape recorder has a pause button and that was helpful because we were initially uncomfortable about just what we'd say and needed time to collect our thoughts.

We settled on reading some short fairy tales and then just talked to her for some minutes. Feeling more relaxed, I began telling her about the night she was born. I had been presenting a workshop in Ohio and calling before I left to board a plane and fly home, found that Meg was in labor. I nearly trampled the other passengers when we disembarked in Minneapolis in my haste to grab a taxi and get to the hospital. Arriving at the hospital, the corridors were dark and quiet and when I reached the birthing room, my first sight was our grandson Kal. Then three months old, he was there with his mother Kate, Meg's sister. I walked in to find Meg still in labor with her husband David and Kate at her bedside. David was holding a cool cloth on her forehead. I told her what David was saying and how quiet Kal was. I said that it was an enchanted evening and the sky was filled with stars and a full moon. I told her about a very kind nurse and how wonderful she was. And then the moment of birth and all the hugs and kisses as we welcomed her into our family. I told her that it was her father who gave her her first bath, how her dimples were discovered and how much she seemed to love the water.

That first tape grew to become a tradition in our family. On every birthday all eight grandchildren get an audiotape from Papa Dick and me. We usually start at the library searching for books appropriate to their age and interests.

The making of a tape has taken on even greater meaning when we began to realize that they are treasured by our grandchildren and listened to over and over again. The more fanciful they are, the more they are enjoyed. Papa Dick started a tape for our grandson Ned when he was seven by banging on pots and pans and announcing what a great day this was!

Grandchildren seem to be most fascinated by family stories. Favorites are how their parents met, their wedding day, their own birth and funny things either they or their parents have said. One favorite tale concerns an episode when our daughter Molly, now the mother of four children, was in first grade and brought home her report card. The teacher made check marks where improvements were called for on an endless variety of behaviors. Molly's teacher had insidiously used a heavy black marker and her report card was filled with checks. I saw it first and I was aghast! I figured Papa Dick could handle this crisis. When he came home from work, I told him that he had a problem. He sat at our kitchen table with the report card laid out in front of him and called Molly into the room. He asked her, "Molly, what do you think of this?" Without a blink, she looked at it and announced, "I DON'T think about it." I remember Papa Dick tossing the report card over his shoulder while we both tried not to laugh.

You can talk on the tapes about things you've noticed about how they've matured during the last year. Since your interest and participation with them will form part of their self-concept, I think it's wonderful to recall some of their finer moments and remark about their talents and interests. We once made a tape for three-year-old Grace who was starting ballet lessons. We played an excerpt from *Swan Lake* and read a story about a little girl in ballet class. Papa Dick has read poetry to his grandsons.

Telling them often how much they are loved is a must for every tape we make and once I suggested that when they feel unloved or misunderstood they might consider playing a tape to remind them again of how their grandparents feel about them. A year or so later, Lucy responded with her own tape. I call it the "Problems Tape." She began with long, drawn out sighs. She continued, "Man am I having problems. WOMAN am I having problems. Maybe part of it is my fault, but I don't want to talk about that part now. You can ask me someday if you really want to know."

When I was in the hospital, feeling a great deal like 'pitiful Pearl', a tape arrived from Mike, Ned, Will and Grace telling me they loved me and hoped I'd soon be feeling better. A person could make a fortune selling that kind of medicine!

I also wonder if someday in the future our great-grandchildren will be listening to the tapes we've made and hearing our voices. Imagine listening to your great grandparents' voices.

A Fleming Fourth of July

What's more exciting than a combination of family and fireworks? Our Fourth of July celebrations took advantage of this, starting gradually and mushrooming with every passing year.

We enjoy spending the Fourth at our cottage. One year, I made pillowcases out of red stripes and blue stars. Further celebration came when we all attended the Lion's Club fireworks display in Stone Lake. It was small town America at its finest. Another year, our daughter Meg brought along face paint as a treat for the children. We all got so involved painting their faces, that we started painting each other's, sometimes with the older children as the artists. Papa Dick had a black eye patch painted on, pirate-like. One of the boys had a flag painted on his face and Rose and Grace had large stars painted around their eyes. We took off for the Stone Lake fireworks in splendid form! Many people smiled or laughed, but a few tried not to look.

Then came the year that David suggested at our Memorial Day Lake Meeting that interested lake people have a parade, using decorated pontoons, small boats, canoes or kayaks. There was general enthusiastic agreement and another lake owner, whose cottage is on an island, suggested we all get together for a picnic on his property following the aquatic parade. The decorated boats would meet at 10:00 on the morning of the Fourth.

We all had a grand time planning what our pontoon would look like and, because we are a family of eaters, much thought went into our picnic lunch. Fried chicken, potato salad, homemade biscuits and lemon bars won out. We decided on the usual red, white and blue streamers and balloons for the boat and everyone wore whatever shorts and tops they had that were red, white and/or blue. As the special attraction, Lucy stood on the front of the pontoon dressed like the Statue of Liberty. She wore a white robe, a gold spray painted cardboard crown and held a spray of plastic stars aloft. Papa Dick put his boombox on the top of the console and played John Philip Sousa marches as loud as he could. We were delighted to find eight other decorated boats that morning with one featuring the Boy Scouts. Everyone wore a Boy Scout uniform and a huge American flag completed their pontoon. They were magnificent!

The following year our five grandsons represented the famous Revolutionary War painting of three young men in their bloody clothes playing a drum, a fife and carrying a flag. I went to Goodwill and bought inexpensive clothes for the boys, tore holes in the garments and put ketchup around the holes for blood. We ripped an old dishtowel in lengths to tie around their heads, also bloodied. Sam brought two drums, Mike a recorder (fife) and Papa Dick located an American flag with a circle of thirteen stars for one of the boys to carry. Papa Dick found a "cat in the hat" stove pipe hat in red, white and blue and wore a white shirt and trousers with a vest made up of small flags.

Lucy—Fourth of July

Another year it was Rose and Grace's turn. Grace's father Gene made large silver stars with glitter that both little girls held with their faces peering out the centers. We found a recording of Lee Greenwood singing *God Bless the USA* along with several other patriotic songs and added those to our recordings of Sousa marches and some lively polka tunes, including the *Beer Barrel* and *She's Too Fat For Me*.

Further inspired thoughts are having Lucy dress as Betsy Ross, sitting on a rocking chair with the flag with thirteen stars and/or Papa Dick himself dressed as John Philip Sousa with a baton. The grandchildren could wear white or light colored slacks with blue shirts that mothers would sew brass buttons on in double rows and hold various instruments that they would pretend to be playing while the marches are blaring from the boombox.

The Fourth of July is a wonderful holiday to celebrate with historical and patriotic events. Even if yours includes a community celebration, add some special family touches to make it even more memorable.

Chapter Four
Grandmother's Zests

Zest is being an artist of everyday life.

— Meg Fleming Sirianni

People who live zestful lives use more of their innate creativity and imagination. I believe they are people who not only think about little surprises or bigger adventures to delight themselves and others, they also take action and make things happen. Many of these people are emotional risktakers and retain something of their childlike awe about their world. They continue to create the anticipation of fun, the actual events and the joyful memories for themselves, their friends and families making memories that grow even sweeter over time.

I have been interviewing people of zest wherever I find them. Many have appeared in workshops I give throughout the country on *Zestful Living*. As I have listened to others and begun to trust my own intuition and artistry a good deal more, my life began to unfold in ways that excited me and gave me an even greater sense of purpose. I borrow freely from the ideas I heard from others with their permission. I love talking to groups about ideas I hear because zest should be passed on and encouraged. Some ideas I've heard required shifts to fit our family.

I've learned a tremendous amount from those closer to home–my four daughters, Papa Dick, my sons-in-law and my nutritious friends. I've read autobiographies about women I admire and learned from their experiences. My mother Harriet was my inspiration, as well. Some I dreamed up myself.

A friendly warning about zest: it becomes addictive! Think of a snowball going downhill, gaining strength and momentum as its speed increases. Think of Dorothy in *The Wizard of Oz*, opening the door to Oz and having her previously black and white world turn into color. It's tapping into more of our senses and, like Lucy, becoming increasingly aware of the possibilities that exist. It's trusting our intuition to help us create the most interesting life we can summon.

My Eclectic and Eccentric Dollhouse

Dollhouses come in countless shapes and sizes. A person could spend a fortune buying the tiny replicas of furniture, wall and rug coverings and decorations many of us can't afford to have in our own homes.

I remember that I had a dollhouse that my father and uncles made during the time they were painting, papering and repairing their parents' old home. They had managed to convince my grandparents to visit another daughter for a week or so and in the midst of their other labor made a dollhouse out of the scraps and leftovers for my sister Ruth and me. There were some wooden pieces of furniture and a shower stall with a cotton curtain my mother must have made.

I wasn't aware I even wanted another dollhouse until I met a woman named Bonnie. For years, Bonnie had collected tiny things gathered from flea markets and garage sales. These treasures found new homes in her handmade dollhouses. We talked about a dollhouse she would build for me and I was tickled when I saw what she put together. Starting with old, sturdy wooden boxes in different sizes, three on the bottom level, two on the second floor and one on the top, she glued buttons along the front edges, glued small sea shells on the bathroom wall and added pieces of gingerbread to make turrets and balconies. Bonnie added miniature paintings cut from magazines and framed on many walls, wallpapered some rooms, and used various colored placemats for rugs. She built tiny shelves and they were filled with little gems. Making a coverlet for a bed out of a napkin and sewing two tiny pillows out of purple and pink satin, Bonnie designed a delightful bedroom. She left most of the rooms bare of furniture for me to fill in as I liked.

Over the last six years I've added some marvelous finds. In the children's playroom I have miniature cars, a train set, rocking horse, a tiny blue teddy bear and a tall masted ship. My finds have included an old black wood stove that brings back warm memories of my grandmother's kitchen, a harp and other musical instruments, a stone fireplace that lights up when plugged in for outdoor cookouts, a family with five children, a dappled horse and black lab, a chamber pot in a cabinet and my prize–a to-scale wooden gazebo that I found on a clearance table at a local department store.

Anything the right size suits this dollhouse and when our grandchildren come they often run to the dollhouse, which is set up in our kitchen, before they take their coats off. They want to see what I've added since their last visit. They (we) play for hours. We make up stories and act them out. I was delighted one day to find all the tables moved out onto the lawn in front of the dollhouse with the family of dolls sitting on little chairs around the tables. I was told they were having a family reunion.

I knew our granddaughters would love the dollhouse and I was pleasantly surprised to find the interest the young boys had in it, as well. I don't have anything they can't touch and breakage of inexpensive things simply doesn't matter.

The Loon on a Lake Table

I was also aware of Bonnie the dollhouse builder's talent of painting fanciful children's furniture. We had a small table and two chairs already so I decided to have her paint them for Rose and Grace who were two years old at the time. I wanted to use them at our cottage. I asked Bonnie to paint a lake on the table with a loon, trees and a canoe. On one chair she painted ROSE with roses and a small lake on the seat and on the other GRACE with suns and a small lake on the seat. Talk about pride of ownership! The girls sit for hours at their table chatting like two older women who have been lifelong friends. Rosie and Gracie, as they call each other, can put their table near the fireplace on rainy days while they color and they always dine there.

Paperdolls With Pizzaz

Lucy is now at an age where many of her friends are playing with paperdolls. Being blind prevents her from knowing what outfit to put on what doll. Wanting to support her independence, I bought a paperdoll book of Southern Belles. I cut them out and then with my handy glue gun glued bits of different fabric and bits of broken jewelry onto the dresses. There were three female dolls and the dresses for each doll had a different "awareness" piece on all the clothes so that Lucy could feel and know what dresses belonged to each doll. A small fabric rose was on all of one of the girl's dresses, for example.

Each of our three granddaughters has a set of paperdolls from the Civil War era and they now plan the dress decorations themselves. This, however, is just the beginning of our fun. Using story fragments from *Gone With The Wind* and my interest in the Civil War, we create mini-dramas after choosing which characters we will be. A particularly fascinating drama was the siege of Vicksburg where we lived in caves during the invasion. Their southern accents are a joy to hear, along with their imaginative words about what that experience must have been like. In one drama, Laura Lee (aka Lucy) gave birth in a cave and the first words her baby said were, "Oh, what did ah say!" an expression Laura Lee became known for throughout our re-enactments.

The Steamer Trunk

Old steamer trunks can be found at flea markets or antique stores for a modest price. Generally, they have about five drawers on the right side and wooden hangers on the left along with a small ironing board and a separate take-out, small suitcase. The outside is made of sheet metal and the inside sometimes is lined with velvet or a tapestry of some kind. Often they have the initials of the original owner on the outside. They have an aura of romance and mystery. They always look as if they must have been a part of a grand adventure, most probably on board an ocean liner sailing to Europe.

As I was cleaning the one I found, I wondered about the woman who originally owned this trunk and where her travels had taken her. Then I started hunting for items to put in the trunk. It would be put in one of the cottage bedrooms and filled with dress-up things for the three little girls. I found a grand array of things at flea markets and the local Goodwill Store. The top drawer is filled with a stash of old costume jewelry and long, elbow-length gloves. The other drawers have funny old hats, shoes, blouses, skirts, dresses and a feather boa. The clothes have been a catalyst for all the granddaughter's imaginations.

Rose has had a crush on her cousin Kal for some time and when I added a bridal veil to the steamer trunk, she was thrilled. Like a nervous bride, she dressed herself up and carefully arranged the veil on her head, with Grace's help. She said, "Do you think Kal will think I'm pretty?" Gingerly, Rose stepped outside the cottage to seek Kal who was madly running around the cottage with his male cousins searching for their walking sticks. I picked up my camera and followed Rose, curious to see his response to her. It warmed a grandmother's heart as he spotted her, rushed over and picked her up in his arms while shouting "My bride!" Rose was enraptured.

On the day the Boot Camp uniforms were handed out to the boys, the three girls were busy at the steamer trunk. Lucy, Rose and Grace put on one outfit after another. Before long they made their grand entrance in their outfit of choice complete with jewelry, hats and shoes. The boys had just responded to Papa's whistle and lined up for inspection. When Dick saw the girls—floozies all–he took me aside and asked if he should include a lecture to the boys on "camp followers!"

Ethel's Fairy House

We bought our cottage several years ago from an elderly woman named Ethel. She was a lovely woman, even writing us a letter after the sale to tell us how nice it would be for her to think of our family enjoying her beloved place. One of our family stories is how the cottage was discovered (*it wasn't for sale*) and purchased (*there was another person determined to buy it and they had deep pockets*) and the anxiously awaited phone call from Ethel telling us that she would sell it to us after receiving Papa Dick's poignant letter with a photo of his four daughters. Sometimes we even read Ethel's letter aloud to further enhance the story.

One summer day, some of the grandchildren decided to build a fairy house. I had a large, woven stick basket that they filled with moss, decorated with ferns, added pine cones for chairs, made a stick table and piled pebbles in a circle for a fireplace, filling the center with red berries representing live coals. It was one of those lazy summer day activities that turns out to be more fun than one would expect, since one thing led to another and the creative juices were flowing. When it was finished, I put it in the screen house and draped little white lights around it. When it was done, Lucy said, "It's Ethel's fairy house. For her spirit to be here with us." And that made it even more special to all of us.

Pillowcases and Placemats

My mother started it all years ago when she made Christmas pillowcases for our four daughters when they were very young. The excitement, after Thanksgiving, when they could put their special pillowcases on, was great. The cases were endowed with special magic and if they thought good thoughts before sleeping, they would be sure to have magical dreams of Christmas. Years later when Molly had the idea of making throw pillows out of the very worn old Christmas pillowcases they loved as children, the idea of special pillowcases surfaced in my brain. Christmas cases first for all the grandchildren, but why not Halloween cases, Green Bay Packer cases for the boys, Fourth of July cases, Welcome Spring cases and special birthday cases? A yard of fabric makes one pillowcase with little effort other than sewing straight.

Making special celebrations out of everyday objects can be delightful. For instance, you can have family calendars made at quick print shops using favorite photographs from previous years. Another use for photos is to have them enlarged to 10 X 16 inches and laminated. They make wonderful placemats. We have a set for everyone in the family for the Fourth of July and a set for each child for Christmas. It does strike me as fun to have everyone's favorite baby photo made into placemats.

Photo Albums Every Christmas

We rarely took photos when our daughters were young. I think I must have been unaware of the swift passage of time, believing life as I knew it would go on forever. Perhaps that's why I'm trying to make up for it now. Guilt is a great motivator. I've been taking a lot of photos for the past ten years or so. Up until last year, I always had doubles made and I'd send some to our daughters throughout the year. Now I save all of them and put them into piles labeled "Anne, Kate, Meg and Molly." Sometime in November, I buy four albums and add the photos. They make a lovely remembrance of the last year and with a little pre-planning it's not much work to do. Why didn't I start this years ago?

Yearly Photo Day

I remember hearing about a family that started taking a specific photo the year their first child was born. It was outside against a background of trees and rocks, creating about five levels. Every following year they took a photo in the same place with the same grouping. The family grew to include six children. As the years passed, the children married and had families of their own. The yearly photo sessions continued as the family has expanded to thirty-two people. Fortunately the setting they originally chose was large enough to include everyone. Imagine having that collection of photos in your family.

We now have a four-year collection, paling by comparison, but a beautiful idea nonetheless. There is a tree on Big Island near our cottage. The tree has fallen and has been held in place by another smaller tree, preventing it from being on the ground or in the water. When such a photo is taken, you need only one person in complete charge who will pass on clothes worn and give orders as to who sits or stands where. It helps if this one person is a grandmother and has a loud voice.

Imagination Boxes

When visiting my daughter Meg's home one day, I noticed a colorful box on her kitchen counter. Her children had decorated the box, gluing bits and pieces of colored paper and ribbons on it. I asked what it was and she told me it was their Imagination Box. Every once in awhile, one of her three children puts their hand into the box and draws out a slip of paper. The children will take turns answering or drawing their response to whatever idea or question they randomly pick. Here's what's in their Imagination Box:

Describe a place that has special meaning for you, a place you really like.

Create an imaginary friend and tell me what they are like and what they look like.

Make three wishes out loud.

Tell me a different ending to one of your favorite stories.

If you could build anything in the world, what would it be?

If you could invent anything, what would it be?

Draw a picture or talk about a dream you've had.

Describe yourself. What do you look like? What do you like about yourself?

What do you suppose it feels like to be an endangered species?

Write a poem about something or somebody you love.

Draw a design using your name.

What is your favorite season? Holiday? Time of day? Weather? Why?

If you were shipwrecked on a desert island, what would you do?

Is it more fun to be a kid or a grown-up? Why?

What is your favorite food? How do you think you would make it?

Pretend you're talking to a person your age who lived over a hundred years ago. What would you tell them about how the world is different now?

If you were a songwriter, what would your song be about?

Tell me about what you think would be the best present anyone could get.

What do you think happens in a zoo at night after the people all go home?

Talk about your favorite sounds, smells or things to touch.

If you could fly, where would you go and what would you do?

Make believe you lived in a treehouse or on the moon or in a cave. What would it be like?

Sit very quietly for a few minutes and tell me what you hear.

I think if interested grandparents had an Imagination Box in their homes, it could lead to some fascinating conversation. Answering the same questions yourself, along with the children, could be great fun, too.

Albert Einstein said, "Imagination is more important than knowledge." Becoming an increasingly zestful grandparent leaks over into other areas of your life as well. What a legacy to leave your children and grandchildren. You might be remembered as the Auntie Mame of your family! Won't they love remembering someone who relished life in all of its color and hues?

CHAPTER *Five*
PASSING THE TORCH

We hold hands with the people in our past and present.

At the start of this book, I included some words from *The Wheel of Fortune* in which Susan Howatch says this: "It's the English who think time is a straight line which can be divided up and parceled out in an orderly fashion, but time isn't like that. Time is a circle, time goes round and round like a wheel and that's why one hears echoes from the past continually...it's because the past is present: you don't have to look back down the straight line, you just look across the circle and there are echoes of the past and the vision of the future. And they're all present, all now...all forever."

Those words speak to me. I do believe time is a circle, that the past is present and we can see visions of the future. We are all part of the people that came before us and we will leave our mark even on those who are yet to be born. It is my hope that the echoes Papa Dick and I leave will instill in our circle a strong sense of family and the certainty of the love we have for each unique individual in that circle. I further hope that each family member, old and young, will have the inner confidence to pursue who they are and what they want in life with the conviction that they have our unconditional support. The stories in this chapter assure me that our family circle is thriving.

At Granny's Side

A few years ago when Papa Dick's mother Dorothy had spent her last nine years in a nursing home, a nurse called to tell us her death was near. She was in a coma when we arrived and Papa Dick and I sat with her for some hours, talking quietly, reading poetry from a Maya Angelou book and holding her hand. Late that morning, I called three of our daughters to let them know what was happening. Our oldest daughter Anne was in Scotland meeting her future husband Steven's family. I told the girls that I would call them if there was any change or when Granny died, but they were to expect her death soon.

I didn't know that after my calls to them that they had called each other and their three cousins Elena, Julie and Mia. Those who could get there planned to meet in Dorothy's room that evening. Julie, who lives in New York, asked that her sisters and cousins call her throughout the evening so that she could feel as much a part of their experience as possible. She told me later that it was very difficult for her not to be there and that she felt she missed an incredible experience. She said that Granny was like their "hub" drawing the seven cousins even closer because of the many years' experience and milestones in their lives witnessed by or shared with Dorothy. Perhaps they were collectively aware that the death of the eldest Fleming matriarch was a significant turning point in each of their lives.

Babysitters had to be quickly recruited for some, but they arrived between eight and nine-thirty in the evening. Papa Dick and I had gone home without knowing what was about to happen.

The five granddaughters came from a four hundred mile radius. Granny was still in a coma when they arrived. The nursing home was quiet and dark. They took turns sitting on her bed and talking to her, sharing memories with each other and Dorothy, finally saying individually what they needed to say. Mia remembers thanking her for two distinct times in her life when Granny was of great support for her. While each woman had their alone time with her, the other four would quietly walk the halls together. Without any of them ever asking for some private time with their grandmother, it was recognized and honored by the others. When they were together in the darkened room, with only the occasional entrance and soft footsteps of the nurses to break the stillness, they talked.

Recalling experiences with her and each other, they cried, smiled and laughed. Molly got herself tangled in the various tubes surrounding Granny when she leaned closer to whisper to her. They each told me of the magnitude of feelings that washed over them that night. Anne and Julie were there, too, because the conversations that took place often involved them. They called Julie on the phone, involving her as much as possible in what was taking place. They talked about their bonds with one another, expressing their feelings for one another and for the woman who no longer would be able to express hers.

In the wee hours of the morning, they left her room. Mia told me that she felt they "released" her, and she died within hours after they left. They all sensed closure and gratitude for the time they spent together.

The following morning Kate, Meg and Molly returned to her room. They were unaware that Granny had died and when they entered her room, the bed had been stripped and the room seemed empty of all the emotion of the evening before. They sat in her room together and then attempted to call Anne in Scotland. Amazingly, they reached her and her three sisters took turns relating their experiences of the hours spent with Granny such a short time ago. Anne, too, became fully aware of what had happened and, for a time, all the miles between them disappeared.

Garden Soup

When nine-year-old Lucy was asked to choose an ancestor and write about this person, she asked for my help. I sent her a list of ancestors with a brief description of each. Several days later she called me to say that she had chosen my fraternal grandmother Lizette Sunderman Decker. I think she was probably influenced when, in my brief description, I referred to her as a saint. She suffered from polio as a child, leaving her somewhat crippled. Lizette went on to give birth to ten children. Throughout her long life she was a cheerful and loving woman. She was a grandmother I adored and spent a lot of time with.

Lucy asked me several questions about her and among those were two that really jogged my memory: "What did she smell like?" and "What did you talk about when you sat on the swing together?" This is the story that Lucy wrote out of my answers to those questions.

Six-year-old Joan Decker sat in her grandmother's garden. The garden took up most of the backyard. It had mostly vegetables, but many flowers. Joan sat arranging some tulips. It was a warm, sunny April morning. The breeze blew a tiny bit and the birds chirped merrily. Joan looked up at the lilac bush. "Pretty soon," she said to herself, "Grandma will have lilacs!"

In a little while, after Joan had finished the tulips and started a vegetable soup, her grandma Lizette Decker came out. Lizette was short and chubby, she had long hair that she always put in a bun. She wore a cotton house dress and a cotton apron, the kind that goes over your head, ties in the back and almost goes to the bottom of the dress. Usually, she smelled of earth from digging in the garden or yeast dough. Right now she smelled of yeast dough. She's been baking bread. As Joan cut vegetables for her soup, she said, "Grandma, would you like to have these red and yellow tulips for the table?" "Yes, please. They're just beautiful," her grandma replied, smiling and taking the tulips from Joan.

"After you finish your soup, we'll have cold potato salad for lunch." Joan loved Lizette's potato salad. It was cold and a little sour. It had potatoes, onions and bacon, it also had a lot of vinegar, that's what made it sour. Joan smiled to herself. Then she started to finish the soup. After she finished the soup of peas, carrots, cucumbers, onions and tomatoes, and lunch, Joan and Lizette sat in the swing, (the swing could fit two people) and talked. They talked about how Lizette missed her mother who lived in Germany and about dreams, too. "What was

Germany like?" asked Joan. "It was beautiful, Joan, very beautiful," Lizette's eyes and voice were distant. Then Lizette brightened. "Germany was a wonderful place!" she said smiling. "I have had many wonderful dreams about Germany."

"Do you think we can make dreams?"

"Well, I don't know, but I think we could."

"So do I. I'd like to try it sometime."

"Yes, sometime we will."

"Maybe we already have made dreams by accident! Do you think we have Grandma?"

"Yes Joan, I think we probably have." Everything about Lizette twinkled and sparkled and glittered, especially her eyes. Lizette's eyes were bright and blue and sparkly and alert. Then they went inside.

While Lizette made dinner, Joan jumped on the feather bed. It was great fun! Joan could imagine she was jumping on a fluffy white cloud Then she played the pump organ in the parlor. Joan didn't take any lessons, but it sounded very pretty. As she played, she could smell the delicious soup and good homemade white bread.

The parlor was a large room, it was shady and cool. It was a long, rectangular room. When you came in, on the back wall was a huge window with a window seat, the window seat had a bright, soft cushion. On the right side stood the large organ, in front of it was a stool that had a velvet cushion. Also on the right side were some chairs and tables, the tables had books and lamps, the chairs matched the stool. On the left side was a couch that matched the stool and chairs. On the walls there were pictures of people in clothes that Joan thought were strange. Girls and women wearing long dresses with lace and ribbon trimmings, and straw hats with ribbons or a veil. Men and boys wearing fancy suits and tall black shiny hats. On the floor was a bright flowered rug. Joan loved the parlor.

Then it was time for dinner, chicken dumpling soup, Joan's favorite food that Lizette cooked. It made Joan feel warm and safe and happy. It made her feel sleepy too, but Joan and Lizette had more plans. When you came into the kitchen, on the back wall, was a big wood stove. There was a cupboard too, filled with everyday dishes and aprons. There was a cupboard for china dishes too and a tea set. That was Joan's favorite cupboard! Lizette would tell Joan where the old china came from.

Then, just before bedtime, they read the dream book. The book was all in German, so Joan couldn't read it. So Lizette read aloud to her. It told what dreams meant. Again Joan wondered, could she make dreams? Had she? Who made good dreams? Who made bad dreams? Joan thought bad dreams were made by a fierce-looking, mean dragon who lived in a musty damp cave. He made the dreams by making a huge bonfire with his fiery breath which was made of the things that make night-mares. Joan also believed that good dreams were made by an older woman. As the woman stirred her magic soup, she takes from her long flowing gown a magic wand made of a lilac. She is the Fairy of Lilac and has many bouquets of lilacs. Her lilacs never died. Her name is Lilac. And in Lilac's wand were all the ingredients for wonderful dreams. As they read, Joan pointed out what was different and what was the same about her theory and the book's. Then Joan went to bed and had a very peaceful sleep.

After words. This is an imaginary day that my grand-ma Joan Decker Fleming spent with her grandma or my great, great grandma, Lizette Sunderman Decker. The story would probably have taken place in the early 1940's. Although this day was imaginary, all the things Joan did with Lizette were things she really did. What Lizette looked like is also true.

The Artists of Everyday Life

A simple memory that will always be with me happened shortly before Christmas many years ago. We were living in Jackson, Mississippi with our two oldest daughters who were then four and two years old. Going home to Wisconsin for the holidays was an ordained decision. Driving nonstop in a Volkswagen "bug" through a snowstorm during the last four hours was the reality. We arrived in my small hometown with an ice encrusted car and a crew of four wearied and disheveled passengers—one requiring an immediate diaper change. Driving down the familiar street we saw my father's welcome. He had made a cardboard waving Santa holding a sign that said, "Merry Christmas, Anne and Kate." It was the most welcoming sight we'd seen. Maybe that's where we first learned how to turn the ordinary into the extraordinary.

From time to time, our grandchildren take ordinary events, things an adult might not consider significant, and write about them. Here are several examples of the budding poets our family has produced.

My grandma should get a special award for just being nice.

My grandma takes me out to movies.

Grandma makes my day better and shines like the sun.

Sometimes she plays bingo and gets really cool prizes like little canoes.

At the cottage she lets me pick out the M&M's from the trail mix.

She plays a game with me called "Ned Wins."

She comes to watch me when my Mom and Dad are gone.

This is why she should win an award.

NED BUTTON

Papa taught me how to drive his ATV!
When I was learning, I drove it straight toward a ditch.
So then I pulled the throttle thinking it was the brake, so it
went faster.
I knew at this speed I could have been hurt bad if I turned
it over.
After that I learned my gears.
I figured that if I had crashed I'd either be dead or ground-
ed for life.
After practicing a little I feel fine and have given a ride to
my Mom and Grandma.
Grandpa is thinking of getting another ATV so that when
I know how to drive I can go on excursions with him in the
woods.
Plus, if he gets to trust me on it and knows that I won't be
a crazy driver
He might let me bring one of my cousins along.

KAL FLEMING

The mountains reached up to the sun
Pulling it under their rough face
The lake danced with life
As the fish jumped and waved goodbye to the day
The trees swayed with sadness
As the sun went to bed behind the dark blanket of night
The sun slowly snuggled up behind the mountains saying
Goodnight to the moon
As it cast its last shadows of day to the ground

MIKE BUTTON

The little bulbs have just woke up
The hyacinth says, "Let us depart."
"Yes," said the tulip. "Let the lovely spring air carry us
out to the place we have longed to be all winter."
"I am filled with joy, indescribable joy," cried the crocus.
Hyacinth put her sweet smell on.
They pushed their way up.

They put on their dresses.
The hyacinth found a perfect place under the apple tree,
next to the shy little crocus.
Let us sing with the birds.
So their voices rose with the birds and made a lovely song.

LUCY SIRIANNI

Kal's Treasure Hunt

When the seeds are planted on fertile soil, they grow. The torch that was lit when Papa Dick lived his Flambeau stories will be held high in the succeeding generations in our family.

Almost a year following our Native American treasure hunt, something took place at the cottage that none of those present will ever forget.

It was June and Kate and Meg, along with their children, were there. Papa Dick would join us later in the day, since it was my sixty-first birthday. Kate's son Kal was the designer of our wondrous look into the heart of a seven-year-old boy.

My daughters and I were drinking coffee and visiting at the kitchen table, keeping our eyes on the four children playing outside on the tire swing. Kal came inside and breathlessly asked for some paper and a pencil. He got what he needed and we all assumed he would again be sketching the trees. We watched as he sat outside on the stone wall and laboriously wrote on pieces of torn paper. We followed him with our eyes as he placed one scrap at a time at the bottom of trees or near rocks. He then disappeared behind the cottage.

After a short time, he called the three of us outside and proudly announced that he had planned a birthday treasure hunt and everybody had to do something. We went outside, coffee cups in hand. It was a mystery to the other children, as well. Kal explained, giving Lucy the first direction verbally. "Take seven big steps from the front door, turn right, take six steps until you find a pine tree. Feel around the bottom of the tree for a piece of paper." She did and Kal said, "Great job, Lucy!"

The next note said "Kate, go twenty-six steps and turn to something red." She did.

"Great job, Kate. This one will be fawed (followed) by Sam. Sam go twenty steps."

"Great job, Sam. Now hand it to Meg. Meg you will find this clue to twenty-two."

"This will be fawed (followed) by Jone (Joan). Go nineteen steps."

As we progressed, getting further directions from Kal as needed, we three women hung back a little and speculated about what the "treasure" would be. Would it be food—a popular compensation in our family–or something he had made or brought with him? None of us remembered Kal searching through the cottage for an article nor did we remember seeing him hide anything in his pockets. We were mystified.

We came to the last of his slips, tucked into the grill of my car. I pulled it out and read, "Great job, all of you! You will find your treasure all around you. LOOK!"

Kal

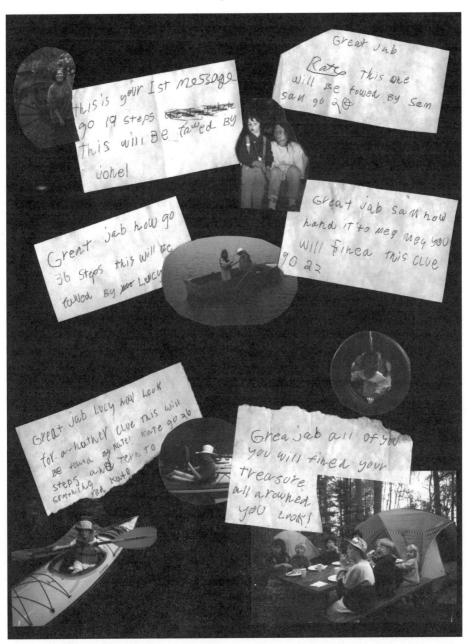

Kal's Clues

Sensing our delight, he then said, "The lake, the cottage, the trees–all of us!"

It was my most memorable birthday and the expressions on our faces, along with some tears, spoke of the pride we have for this young man. Kal and his cousins Mike, Ned, Will, Grace, Lucy, Sam and Rose will be the keepers of the flame. I have complete faith in all of them.

Afterword

In my workshops, I often speak of Anne Morrow Lindbergh and her words in *Gift From the Sea:* "Many people are trying, like me, to evolve another rhythm in their lives, with more creative pauses in it, more adjustment to their individual needs, and new and more alive relationships to themselves as well as others." I believe the "rhythm" of our lives is largely an outcome of the choices that are ours to make.

In the end, the only thing that really matters is the relationships we have with those we love. One day recently, our grandson Sam said, "The word our family says the most is FOOD!"

It is my deepest desire that the word our family feels the most is LOVE. I hope that your position in your family circle will be one that will be remembered with joy for all the worthwhile memories you created while spending time with those you love.

Joan and Dick

WITH APPRECIATION

I want to express my gratitude to three women who, each in her own way, has given me strong emotional support during the writing of this book. Johanna Warloski is my friend and her belief in my vision has never wavered. Her own father was a superb grandfather. Among the many things he did, with and for his grandchildren, was to create a *Family Cabinet* in which he gathered memorabilia and photos...all of which were connected to family stories and history. It was his pleasure to gather his grandchildren around the cabinet and give them a deeper sense of their identity.

Mary Taylor is a true friend who wouldn't allow me to quit when I was discouraged. Her ability to sharpen my focus and "keep on keeping on" was essential to my progress. Her father was a creative and generous grandfather. A poet himself, he was a prodigious reader and outdoor man...a true renaissance man. How he loved to guide his grandchildren and instill in them a passion for life!

Mary Bradley Grewe is a friend who has taught me courage and unconditional love between friends that I will always treasure. Her enthusiasm for family adventures is as strong as my own. Her father was a beloved grandfather. With a bear skin draped over his shoulders, he hid among the trees to delight them when they were due to arrive for a visit at his summer home. Every photo and family treasure that he passed on to his children and their children was carefully labeled either with the names and dates or a brief history of where a particular treasure was acquired. Their sense of family runs deep.

I also want to thank my editor and friend Barbara Winter for her insight, her questions for me and her marvelous enthusiasm when we both agreed I was saying exactly what I wanted to say. Her empathy often allowed us to be of one mind.

Thanks to Kathleen Olson for her photography. She is greatly talented with an eye both for the playful and imaginative.

Debbie Fleming Caffery took the photos of Papa Dick on the swing and the two of us at the end of the book.

Thanks, also, to Milt Adams whose grandparents raised him and believed he was perfect. They were right. He was the perfect publisher.

Finally, I want to thank my own father for his grandfathering, for he too was among the ones who cared about the legacy he would leave.

ABOUT THE AUTHOR

Joan Decker Fleming is a seminar leader and author as well as a grandmother of nine lively children. For the past twenty-five years she has conducted seminars around the country for clients that include Northwestern Mutual, Nordstrom, and the Sales and Marketing Executives. She is also a trainer for the *Seven Habits of Highly Effective People* and has worked extensively with numerous women's groups.

Joan loves to read and gets her best ideas when walking. As the mother of four daughters she has fantasized about writing a modern version of *Little Women*. A resident of rural Eau Claire, Wisconsin, she would rather swim than cook.

I'D LOVE TO HEAR FROM YOU

I would enjoy hearing from you and reading a story from your family. When I think of the wealth of stories that are out there, I am convinced that we have much to learn from each other's experiences. Let us form a collective voice and give meaning to family values. Write to me at:

8705 Rambil Road,
Eau Claire, WI 54703.

You can order additional copies of this book from the same address. Please make checks payable to Joan Fleming and add $2.00 for shipping and handling.

If you want further information about my workshops, *Zestful Living!, Zestful Women!* or *The Seven Habits of Highly Effective People*, call me at 800-750-2415.